Women in Higher Education:
A Contemporary Bibliography

Kathryn M. Moore
with *Peter A. Wollitzer*

Prepared by The Pennsylvania State University
University Park, Pennsylvania 16802

Published by The National Association of Women Deans,
Administrators and Counselors
Washington, D.C. 20036

Preface

After teaching a seminar on academic women for three years, it became apparent that a great deal of research on this topic was underway but also that much of it was isolated, disconnected, hence ineffectual in providing any summative assessment of women's roles and experiences in academia. It was time to see where all the effort, activity and, in some cases, supportive funding had brought us. The present collection of research reflects the enormous increase in scholarly interest and activity related to women's educational and career experiences. Taken as a whole, the research affords a self-conscious assessment of how well women and collegiate institutions are doing in their renewed effort to equalize the educational opportunities and advantages upon which so much of our American career and social structure is hinged.

The outcome of our assessment shows that there has been a dramatic increase in both the quantity and the quality of research on academic women in the period covered by this Bibliography, 1970 to the present. However, additional and better conceptualized research remains a pressing need. It is our hope that this publication will encourage individuals of both sexes and in the various disciplines to undertake the challenges that such research provides not only for the sake of the research itself but also because postsecondary education and society generally will benefit.

We would like to thank a number of people for their assistance and support of the project. Kenneth P. Mortimer, Director of the Center for the Study of Higher Education, provided both scholarly and financial support for the Project from its inception. Jane E. McCormick, former President of NAWDAC, served as liaison to the organization and superb facilitator throughout. Frank Sherman accessed the entries on the computer and carried out the technical preparation in its various stages. Finally, we wish to thank Mary Ann D. Sagaria, research assistant at the Center, who carried the work through the final, critical stages to completion. Her expertise and devotion to the work are greatly appreciated.

Kathryn M. Moore
University Park, Pennsylvania

Peter A. Wollitzer
Chicago, Illinois

About the Authors

Kathryn M. Moore is Associate Professor and Research Associate a the Center for the Study of Higher Education at Penn State. She received the degrees of B.A./B.S. and M.A. in Higher Education from the Ohio State University and her Ph.D. in Educational Policy Studies from the University of Wisconsin. Prior to coming to Penn State, she worked as Assistant to the Associate Dean of the College of Letters and Science at the University of Wisconsin and as Assistant Professor of Higher Education at Cornell University. While at Cornell, she served as coordinator of the Counseling and Student Personnel Program for two years. She has published and taught on such topics as the history of higher education, the college student, and academic women. She is a member of the National Advisory Council for the ERIC Clearinghouse on Higher Education and the Pennsylvania Planning Committee for ACE's National Women's Leadership Identification Program and the National Association of Women Deans, Administrators and Counselors.

Peter A. Wollitzer is Program Officer at the Institute of European Studies in Chicago, Illinois. From 1976 to 1978 he was a doctoral candidate and research assistant in higher education at the Center for the Study of Higher Education of the Pennsylvania State University. Before coming to Penn State, he served two years as Assistant to the Director of the University of California's Study Center in Paris. His principle areas of interest are international and comparative dimensions of higher education, and while at the Center he has published in these and other areas. Mr. Wollitzer earned his B.A. with high honors at the University of California, Santa Barbara, and his M.A. at the University of California, Berkeley, and his Ed. D. at Penn State.

Contents

Preface iii
About the Authors iv
Contents v

Chapter One
Overview of the Research
    by Kathryn M. Moore 1

Methodological Notes
    by Peter A. Wollitzer 5

Chapter Two
Academic Women: Historical and Contemporary Perspectives
    Introduction 7
    Historical Perspectives 8
    Contemporary Perspectives 12

Chapter Three
Academic Women: Students
    Introduction 15
    Role Behavior 16
    Careers 21
    College/Student Interactions 28
    Adult Women in Higher Education 32
    Discrimination 36
    Achievement Behavior and Persistance 40
    Minority Women 42
    Characteristics of Women Students 43
    Counseling Women Students: Tools and Techniques 46
    College Women and Sports 48
    Women in Specific Majors 49
    Rates of Return 51
    Entire Journal Issues 52

Chapter Four
Academic Women: Graduate Students

Introduction 55
Psychosocial Factors in Women's Graduate Study 56
Placement and Career.. 58
Institutional Structures 60
Training in Specific Fields... 61

Chapter Five
Academic Women: Administrators

Introduction 65
Discrimination.. 66
Roles and Characteristics 68
Leadership Development 69
Miscellaneous 71

Chapter Six
Academic Women: Faculty

Introduction 73
Discrimination.. 74
Strategies and Instruments Related to Discrimination
   and its Reduction 80
Women in the Disciplines.. 85
Women Academics vs. Men Academics:
   Traits, States, and Productivity 91
General Studies 94

Chapter Seven
Bibliographies and Demographic Studies

Introduction 99
Bibliographies.. 100
Demographic Studies 102
Institutional and Geographically Delimited Studies....................... 104

Index 109

CHAPTER ONE

Overview of the Research

Kathryn M. Moore

In 1979, there can be no question that concern with the place of women in the academic world is needed. Since scholarly attention to any issue must begin with a thorough knowledge of the existing, relevant research and writing, one of our intentions in creating this Bibliography was to facilitate the initial literature review process required of future researchers in this field. Another important intention was to take stock of the research and activity to date in such a way that trends and patterns in the literature could be distinguished, and areas needing further attention defined.

When a topic spans many disciplines, as this one does, it is often not the topic itself, but rather a disciplinary base which forms the motive of inquiry. Hence some of the research included below used academic women as the object of the study, but not its chief *raison d'etre*. Breakthroughs in knowledge are frequently attributable to such connections between an old discipline and a new subject area, and women are not the first to benefit from such discipline-based or theoretical approaches. Our quest for relevant research did not penetrate any one discipline beyond those studies pertaining specifically to women in higher education, although many excellent works within such disciplines as history, psychology, and sociology contribute importantly to research on academic women.

Looking at the whole of the work assembled in the bibliography one cannot help sensing the excitement, passion and thrill of discovery that the research represents. Here are hundreds of able, often beginning researchers, mostly women, engaged in an endeavor that can be likened to the discovery of a new continent so little has previously been known or studied about women and so much assumed. These researchers have finally broken with the silent conspiracy that women are not a fit subject for scholarly inquiry. And now that the ground has been broken, money is also coming to finance the research and the implementation of findings that flow from it. We are encouraged by the number of excellent studies we uncovered. Far from being a mere flash in the scholar's pan, the quality and quantity indicate that research on women will continue to flourish.

The research entries were categorized under seven topic chapters delineated primarily according to the various roles women hold in higher education, from student through faculty and administrator. Within these categories, the research was organized according to concepts or research areas derived largely from an inspection of the research itself. That is, we imposed no abstract categories within the chapters, but rather attempted to reflect the groupings that occurred naturally. Of course, these subcategories are of our own devising; the research undoubtedly could be grouped in other ways. Our hope, however, is that the bibliography will be self-explanatory and provide accessibility to the separate entries without difficulty. Readers are referred to the Methodological Notes and to the introductory section that precedes every chapter.

We decided to confine our search to research published from 1970 onward because we felt excellent bibliographies existed for earlier periods and also because we sensed a burgeoning of research since 1970. In fact, our listing includes some 400 separate entries. Of necessity we picked an arbitrary cut-off date of January 1978, although many excellent new pieces continue to reach us.

Among the seven major categories, the bulk of research has focused on *Women as Students*. The least researched categories are the history of women's higher education and women as administrators. Within the category of women as students, much of the research has followed traditional lines of inquiry used in studying new students. In our view, this has been an acceptable initial strategy since it has served as a corrective to the implicit assumption of previous research that what was true for men students probably applied to women. The new research points out that such an assumption is far too simplistic.

One problem with the research on women students is that it is based almost exclusively on the four-year college. The studies of students, male or female, which have two-year colleges or other post-secondary educational enterprises as an institutional base are few. This is particularly regrettable since the majority of students now attend institutions of other types than four-year colleges and in other modes than regular, full-time attendance.

New and growing areas of research are developing on women students as minorities, as adults, and as athletes. All of these are in the exploratory, descriptive stages, and few have yet produced any new conceptual insights. However, let us hope the second wave of research on women in these categories can begin to work from more conceptual bases.

Academic Women in Historical and Contemporary Perspective was a chapter we established in the hope that useful works could be cited that effectively describe and analyze the contexts in which women encounter higher education and the changes that have occurred over time. For the most part, those dealing with the contemporary scene accomplished our objective with considerable insight and flare. Regrettably, research on women's educational past is less well represented, but we have the distinct impression that a good deal is being done in the form of dissertations that may soon find their way into the professional, published media. Our anticipation is tempered somewhat by the knowledge that competition is fierce for space in today's historical and social science journals, and that the publication of books, especially by university presses, has become increasingly difficult due to financial stringencies. In short, the historical section was one in which we were most strongly tempted to include dissertations and for which we urge additional research.

The study of *Graduate Students* has never been closely investigated, but since 1960 studies on this topic have increased in number. Doctoral study is a crucial phase for women. Many who have excellent records as undergraduates and even as masters candidates do not persist in doctoral work. Special circumstance appear to exist in this academic phase which operate to diminish women's opportunity. Research in this area spells out rather carefully what these constraints are, and more research is welcome.

Academic Women as Faculty is a growing area of inquiry. Jesse Bernard's book, *Academic Women* is the pioneer work. Recent research has focused on the many complexities and constraints that women who aspire to faculty status undergo. The large number of affirmative action generated studies repeat again and again for various institutions and disciplines the simple fact: women are discriminated against as faculty. Their mobility, promotion rates, salaries, access to research and opportunity networks, all are invariably subject to discrimination. In the past such discrimination was an open and widely accepted, if not expressly endorsed, practice. Today the situation has become more complex, highly subtle, and circuitous but nevertheless discrimination against women persists. Particularly important avenues of research are those dealing with the structure and politics of the research activity itself. That is, how ideas are developed, funded and disseminated; how the informal social networks among which ideas and scholars circulate actually function. Only by studying the constraints women researchers encounter as outsiders to this system has there been any effort to reform access routes for the mutual benefit of men and women scholars alike.

Taken as a whole, the research encompassed in this section on faculty provides as much a measure of shifts in academic perception as a measure of actual change in structure. Of course, higher education has changed enormously in the past two decades, but only as the pressures of equal opportunity and financial stricture developed did people inside and outside academe begin to take full measure of the extent of that change.

Women as Administrators is an area of research that remains largely unexplored. The effective studies that do exist borrow heavily from management and complex organization studies based on industry and government. Little is actually known, though much is presumed, about women's behavior in positions of academic leadership and responsibility. Certainly the operant assumption has been that there are differences and that they reflect negatively upon women. It must also be acknowledged that the number of women holding such positions has been few, and they have been closely confined to a small number of positions and a narrow group of institutions single sex or religious colleges. Hence the opportunity to study women administrators in numbers and contexts similar to men has not been and still is not available. Equally constrained are the research concepts and questions being used. A great deal of research focuses on traits and states, while very little has been done to analyze the structure(s) within which higher education leadership arises and/or operates. In short, full scale research on women as academic administrators remains to be undertaken. Until it is, knowledge of such women must go a'borrowing to other types of settings or forms of research.

This brief overview of the findings contained in our bibliography suggests new directions for research:
1. We need a better understanding of the history of women's higher education. More studies of individual women leaders and scholars, and more studies of women's experiences in various time periods and at various institutions are all greatly needed.

2. More sophisticated research on the dynamics of women's educational experiences as students is called for, including a greater sensitivity to the multiplicity of roles and influences women experience.
3. We need to understand more fully the ways in which the structure of higher education affects the development of women in their various roles as students, scholars, and administrators. This should include analysis of the dynamics between institutional structure and the individual women and its effect on values, attitudes and behaviors.
4. A greater emphasis on analytic and evaluative as opposed to descriptive research is needed. More attention must be given to the effects of various programmatic attempts at providing equity, and to evalutaions of the outcomes for the institution and the individual. Palliative as opposed to effective efforts need to be identified and reformed.
5. Further exploration of the development of intellect as it relates to women must be undertaken. We need to understand how higher education as a system both perpetuates and also frustrates (or screens) the development of ideas, and how these functions relate to higher education's role as a major access route to society's occupational structure. These interconnections are not well studied, but women's desire for access to both idea-making within academia and to occupations outside it provide impetus for such studies.

This bibliography joins a brief but distinguished collection of bibliographies on women and education. We are particularly indebted to the work of Helen S. Astin and her associates. Their volume, *Women: A Bibliography of Their Education and Careers* is an examplar of thorough scholarship. It is our hope that our efforts will be as useful to scholars and students of women as the others have been to us.

Methodological Notes

Peter A. Wollitzer

The process of compiling this bibliography began with an outline of major topical areas to be covered: historical and contemporary perspectives on academic women, and academic women as undergraduates, graduate students, faculty members, and administrators. These basic designations remained throughout the processes of compilation, revision, and reorganization although they were modified and expanded to their present form along the way.

Our criteria for inclusion of citations were essentially three: that items fit the above categories at least loosely, qualify as research (although not necessarily empirical research), and have a publication date no earlier than 1970. From the contents of the bibliography it is clear that we strayed slightly from the ideal to include, occasionally, works of significance published prior to 1970 as well as seminal non-research items which we considered indispensible to a bibliography on academic women. Because most entries date from 1970 or later, we did take care to note those items with good bibliographies of the earlier literature on academic women.

Primarily for reasons of inaccessibility, we decided against including dissertations. Appropriate publications emanating from dissertation research were included, however. There do appear to be numerous recent dissertations in the topical areas covered by this bibliography, and readers interested in these are referred to *Dissertation Abstracts*.

The identification of sources began with an extensive search of the Educational Resources Information Center (ERIC) system and the Social Science Citation Index for the period 1970–1978. Leads resulting from the bibliographies of appropriate items were then pursued. The most recent literature was searched source by source, proceeding essentially from the authors' knowledge of and familiarity with appropriate sources, and the senior author's previous research on academic women. Numerous ERIC citations were used, with permission, either *in toto* or in edited form. In other cases where abstracts were borrowed, they are so noted.

CHAPTER TWO

Academic Women: Historical and Contemporary Perspectives

Introduction

Historical research on academic women is a fledgling research area at this point in time, as evidenced by our inclusion of only seventeen entries.

Two of the entries, Burstyn (1973) and Graham (1975), concern themselves principally with the historical research itself, the former assessing it and the latter attempting to guide its future.

Most of the remaining entries deal with the question of access in its traditional sense or in a broadened interpretation of the term. Conway (1974) to some extent and Smith (1975) to a greater extent expand the meaning of access in bringing to light the exclusion of women from the very means of creating and structuring knowledge. This exclusion has limited women's access to social institutions not only at the relatively superficial level regulated by codes and rules, but at the level of thought itself. Roby's findings support this view, while the remaining items relate historical attempts and events tending to rectify the imbalance.

The essays and "think pieces" grouped under the small but important cluster on contemporary perspectives provide an opportunity to consider reflectively — before turning on the empirical floodlights that characterize most entries in this bibliography — what Cynthia Epstein has appropriately termed "Woman's Place," and how it is both changing and remaining the same.

Historical Perspectives

Bernard, J. *Academic women.* University Park, PA: The Pennsylvania State University Press, 1964.

> Directed toward exploring life in academia as a woman, the "invisible rules" which restrict her movements, and the cultural roles which have interfered with her achievements and progress. Points out the notion of "freedom to fail." Statistical in nature.

Burstyn, J.N. Women and education: A survey of recent historical research. *Education Leadership,* 1973, *31*(2), 173–177.

> A short "state of the art" assessment of historical research on women in higher education with special focus on new research and study involving nineteenth century developments.

Carnegie Commission on Higher Education. *Making affirmative action work in higher education.* San Francisco: Jossey-Bass, 1975.

> An extensive study of the academic policies affected by affirmative action. The study includes historical information on the federal policies, the timetable set to meet these objectives and the deficiencies in the administration of these policies.

Conway, J.K. Coeducation and women's studies: Two approaches to the question of women's place in the university. *Daedalus,* 1974, *103*(4), 239–249.

> An excellent critical historical analysis of the development of coeducation in American higher education and what it means. Conway argues that access is only one element of equitable social opportunity for women; changes in the curriculum, the opportunity to participate in the creation of knowledge (see also Smith, 1975), and the potential for subsequent career development must all be considered. To date, they have been considered lightly if at all.

Frankfort, R. *Collegiate women.* New York: New York University, 1977.

> Examines the lives of five important women leaders in nineteenth century higher education, including Alice Palmer, M. Carey Thomas and Ellen Richards.

Freeman, J. *Women on the social science faculties since 1892.* Washington, D.C.: American Political Science Association, 1969. [ERIC ED 041567]

> This study is concerned with the position of women on the social science faculties in the graduate division of the University of Chicago. The history and experience of several women faculty members in the various social science departments are reviewed. A few generalizations can be drawn: (1) few women are hired and few stay more than the length of one appointment (3 years); (2) the first appointment is usually that of instructor or lecturer, rather than assistant professor; (3) those who stay generally remain in untenured positions for an abnormally long time; and (4) those who become full professors do so by rising through the "women's departments" or are brought in from other universities at a tenured position. The appendix includes a list of the women on the social sciences faculties 1892–1968 as listed in the graduate catalogs, fellowships given in the social sciences by sex, and tables on the numbers of men and women faculty members, by rank and salary, and on the number of students by sex in the college, the graduate school and degrees awarded.

Freivogel, E.F. The status of women in the academic professions. *The American Archivist,* 1973, *36*(2), 183–202.

> A contemporary history of women in academic professions, with emphasis upon the role of various disciplinary associations in advancing the status of academic women.

Graham, P.A. So much to do: Guides for historical research on women in higher education. *Teacher's College Record,* 1975, *76*(3), 421–429.

> Reviews the nature of existing historical research on women in higher education, examines the consequences of writing women's history, and suggests areas needing further research attention, such as the influence of college on women as students and the role of sororities.

Graham, P.A. *Women in higher education: A bibliographical inquiry, 1974.* [ERIC ED 095742]

> The history of higher education in the U.S. traditionally has been characterized by the same kinds of studies as most other American history: ones that focus on the experiences or concerns of the authors. What such history ignores is the group that for most of this century comprised about 40 percent or more of the undergraduate student body and about 20–25 percent of the faculties; namely, women. The difficulty of looking at the history of women in higher education through the same methodological lens as men is that the focus on success brings forth a set of women that is significantly different from the other women educators and from other women. Investigations of back-

grounds of successful women faculty and administrators suggests that many of these women have had one of two experiences: attending an all-girl's high school or college or coming from an immigrant family. In single sex institutions, a teacher can support and encourage her students vigorously in a fashion that is rare in coeducational institutions where both faculty and students often tend to regard male students as more meritorious of academic consideration. Other areas that need further study concerning women are discussed, including the influence of sororities, the role of the academic wife, influence of college life on women students, effects of coeducational institutions on women, and sex-linked curricula.

Helson, R. The changing image of the career woman. *Journal of Social Issues*, 1972, *28*(2), 33–45.

Helson, R. The changing image of the career woman. *Journal of Social Issues*, 1972, *28*(2), 33–45.

This is an historical look at the 1950s view that women can work *if* family comes first. It is also a review of today's deemphasis of motherhood and new focus on the career development of women.

Holmstrom, E.I. *Educational development of American women: A historical view.* Paper presented at the Symposium on the Development of Women through History, International Society for the Study of Behavioral Development, Ann Arbor, Michigan, August 1973. [ERIC ED 093232]

This historical review describes the educational development of women in higher education. Emphasis is placed on 1) the beginning of formal education for women, secondary and higher education, and 2) higher education and the twentieth century.

McGuigan, D.G. *A dangerous experiment: 100 years of women at the University of Michigan.* Ann Arbor, Michigan: University of Michigan Center for Con-'tinuing Education for Women, 1970. [ERIC ED 047609]

The history of women's struggle to gain admission to the University of Michigan beginning with the first female applicant in 1858, admission of a female in 1870, descriptions of who could come to an all-male college, the obstacles they met, and what they chose to do with their education. The reaction against coeducation in the early 1900's (quota systems) is disucussed, along with a statement on the status of women in academia in 1970.

Owens, N.J. Higher education for women: An American innovation. *Phi Kappa Phi Journal,* 1977, *57*(1), 16–8.

>Advances in higher education for women are reviewed: 1) since colonial times; 2) during the emergence of female academies; and 3) as a result of the establishment of land grant colleges.

Roby, P. Women and American higher education. *Annals of the American Academy of Political and Social Science,* 1972, *404*, 118–139.

>An historical treatment of higher educational opportunities for women in the U.S. The major emphases are 1) that development of opportunities have been closely tied to the economy's need for females with particular skills and to the financial needs of colleges and universities, and 2) that higher education reflects the "competitive, egotistical, and entrepreneurial culture to which men have been socialized."

Sandler, B. Sex discrimination, admissions in higher education and the law. *College and University,* 1975, *50*(3), 197–212.

>An historical look and contemporary analysis of 1) sex discrimintion in higher education admissions; 2) how Title IX of the 1972 Educational Amendments affects such discrimination.

Smith, D.E. An analysis of ideological structures and how women are excluded: Considerations for academic women. *Canadian Review of Sociology and Anthropology,* 1975, *12*(4), 353–369.

>This article stipulates that women have been and continue to be "excluded from the production of the forms of thought, images, and symbols in which their experience and social relations are expressed Established knowledges and modes of thinking therefore automatically constitute women as objects. Disciplines must rethink and reconstitute existing knowledge and thought.

Tournier, M. Women and access to university in France and Germany (1861–1967). *Comparative Education,* 1973, *9*(3), 107–117.

>This study traces the development of women's access to higher education in France and Germany, compares the two countries on this issue, and attempts to interpret the findings in light of the particular cultural/historical context of each country. Economic, political, and psychological factors are considered.

Contemporary Perspectives

Astin, H.S., Cartter, A.M. & Hirsch, W.Z. (Eds.) *Women — A challenge to higher education*. New York: Praeger, 1977.

> Recent efforts to assess the impact of women on higher education have been relatively few. This volume brings together eleven eminent scholars who examine the role women have played in shaping higher education. Divided into three sections, the first part traces the educational leadership of women from the founding of women's colleges through the recently established programs in women's studies, and also considers the present role of women as students and educators. Part II summarizes the employment patterns of women entering the labor market. Part III discusses the issues and challenges confronting educated women with regard to social responsibility and public policy.

Chalmers, E.L., Jr. Achieving equity for women in higher education graduate enrollment and faculty status. *The Journal of Higher Education*, 1972, *43*(7), 517–524.

> Good expository article addressing the "why" of the disproportionate representation of men in higher education. Lower levels of feminine expectation, the use of criteria better adapted to the needs and lifestyles of men, and the unfair application of fair criteria are identified as focal points of discussion and debate in efforts toward the achievement of equity for women in higher education.

Epstein, C.F. *Woman's place*. Berkeley, CA: University of California Press, 1970.

> Why women, especially those who are well educated, underperform, underachieve, and underproduce is the focus of this important book.

Freeman, J. Women's liberation and its impact on campus. *Liberal Education*, 1971, *57*(4), 468–478.

> A provocative essay on women's opportunities in a man's world, what to do about it and what not to do.

Furniss, W.T. & Graham, P.A. *Women in higher education*. Washington, D.C.: American Council on Education, 1974.

> The analyses and suggestions of thirty-eight leaders in education, feminism, foundations, law, and government are collected to set contexts for decisions

facing colleges and universities concerning women students faculty members, and administrators. Among the issues are affirmative action, academic programs, accountability, equality, and equity. Most of the authors say it is the conscious and unconscious practices and prejudices of men that hinder women in their endeavors. Impediments to motivation, productivity, and careers, and the cost effectiveness of women professionals are discussed in detail by several experts.

Howe, F. (Ed.). *Women and the power to change*. New York: McGraw-Hill, 1975.

An important collection of four essays which analyze the male-dominated university from the points of view of four different kinds of academic women: a poet, a sociologist, an attorney, and a humanist. Particular emphasis is placed upon the power that men, through law and tradition, are able to exercise over the lives of women.

Oltman, R.M. *The evolving role of the women's liberation movement in higher education*. Washington, D.C.: American Association of University Women, 1971. [ERIC ED 049489]

While increasing numbers of women are attending college today, their professional opportunities remain limited and many types of discrimination exist. A major thrust to improve the role of women in academe is developing from diverse sources, and one of these efforts is a survey conducted by the American Association of University Women (AAUW) to document aspects of the role of women in higher education. Results support the growing data that women do not have equal status with men in academe. At every level - student body, administration, faculty, and trustees - women are underrepresented or placed in positions with little power.

Robinson, L.H. *The status of academic women*. Washington, D.C.: ERIC, 1971. [ERIC ED 048523]

This report on the status of academic women is divided into three parts. Section 1 presents a review of 4 major research studies that collectively provide a comprehensive description of academic women. The studies are: "Academic Women," by Jesse Barnard, "The Woman Doctorate in America," by Helen Astin, "Women and the Doctorate," by Susan Mitchell, and "Women as College Teachers," by Jean Henderson. The specific criteria most frequently used by investigators to assess the status of academic women are also discussed. Section 2 consists of 54 annotated campus reports that cover employment conditions for women at 65 institutions of higher education. The third section describes 25 projects covering the establishment of committees task forces, and study groups by professional associations specifically to collect and disseminate information on employment conditions for women at various institutions and within specialized fields.

Stiehm, J. (Ed.). *The frontiers of knowledge*. Los Angeles, CA: University of Southern California Press, 1976.

> A collection of autobiographical essays by six accomplished women professionals who tell how they reached their profession, how their work is conducted, and where the limits of their respective professional fields lie. The essays are introduced by the editor as first bringing pleasure; second, providing inspiration; and third, providing instruction through example.

Women on campus: 1970: A symposium. Ann Arbor, MI: University of Michigan Center for Continuing Education for Women, 1971. [ERIC ED 054723]

> The symposium, Women on Campus, 1970, held at the University of Michigan centered on three major topics: "Toward a New Psychology of Women", "The Case of the Women Graduate Student": and "The University and Women." The papers that were presented concerning the first topic included: "Internal Barriers to Achievement in Women — an introduction," by Elizabeth Douvan; "Psychological and Psychosomatic Responses to Oral Contraceptive Use," by Judith Bardwick; "The Motive to Avoid Success and Changing Aspirations of College Women," by Matina Horner; and "Differential Impact of College on Males and Females," by D. Diane Hatch. Papers presented on the second topic included: "The Woman Graduate Student in Sociology," by Greer Litton Fox; "Graduate Women in Political Science — A Recent Research Study," by Sybil Stokes; "Discrimination and the Women Law Student," by Noel Anketell Kramer; "The Black Woman Graduate Student," by Grace E. Mack; and "A Graduate in Population Planning Looks at the Future of Women," by Carolyn Houser. The two papers on the last topic were: "Reflections on the Future of Universities and of University Women," by Charles H. Tilly; and "Change for Women — Glacial or Otherwise," by Jean W. Campbell. Some recent research on women at Michigan is included in the report.

CHAPTER THREE
Academic Women: Students

Introduction

Research pertaining to women students comprises by far the largest portion of the recent research on women in higher education. An alarmingly small part of it is conceptually-based, however, and that which is appears to rely on a very limited conceptual repertoire. "Fear of success," for example, pervades much of the recent work in feminine socialization and applied role theory, including career aspiration and vocational behavior, but little else is seen.

We have clustered the recent research on women students under a number of subheadings, but in this chapter of the bibliography more than the others, there is overlap among the clusters. To some extent this overlap may be attributed to the reliance of researchers on such a limited conceptual repertoire.

The largest clusters are those entitled, *Role Behavior* and *Careers*. *Role Behavior* includes entries on role perception, role conflict, feminine socialization, and fear of success, and suggests strongly that traditional expectations about feminine roles - both personal and societal - substantially influence women at every step along the way to, through, and beyond higher education. The cluster entitled *Careers* overlaps susbtantially with *Role Behavior* and covers the question of careers both from the point of view of l) the individual's aspirations, choice, and vocational behavior, and 2) the job market that is available to women.

Also substantial in size are the clusters we have called *College/Student Interactions, Adult Women in Higher Education,* and *Discrimination*. Entries in the first of these clusters deal with the variety of ways in which certain kinds of collegiate environments and programs affect women students, and vice-versa. Several of them deal with the issue of women's colleges vs. coeducational colleges, and at least one deals with the case of women in two-year colleges specifically. Entries clustered under the heading *Adult Women in Higher Education* cover the field broadly - if not deeply - from the needs and aspirations of reentering women, to programmatic considerations about filling those needs. Astin's new collection on adult women and higher education also assesses the impacts of programs now in operation. Finally, the cluster we have called *Discrimination* comprises a potpourri of entries which document, classify and analyze discrimination against women students. Two very recent statistical insights (Leslie, 1977 and Magarell, 1978) are included to show that progress in the domain of anti-discrimination is being made. Especially useful are Ekstrom's three categories of barriers to participation of women in higher education which lend some order to the otherwise rather imprecise issue of "discrimination."

Much smaller in size are the miscellaneous clusters we have called *Achievement Behavior and Persistence, Minority Women, Characteristics of Female Students,*

Counseling Tools and Techniques, College Women and Sports, Women by Field of Study, and *Rates of Return to Women Students.*

Items under the first subheading address differences in *motivation and achievement* between men and women, as well as correlates among achievement, persistence, and motivation in women. One entry (Hewitt and Goldman, 1975) disputes the oft-cited observation that women overachieve compared to men, attributing the observed differences to differential patterns of male and female enrollment in easier vs. harder majors. The cluster on *Minority Women* deals with the status, aspirations, and motive to avoid success of Black women, while the cluster on *Characteristics* describes women students in general from a research perspective.

Under *Counseling Tools and Techniques* are included a good review of the research on counseling tools and programmatic considerations. Entries in the very limited section on *Women in Sports* introduce the salient issues and describe the situation in collegiate athletics. The section on *Women by Field of Study* is dominated by studies originating in the engineering fields, with very few studies appearing in other academic areas.

Finally, four entries on *Rates of Return* are included here. These studies disagree on the relative value, economic and otherwise, of women's participation in higher education.

At the end of this section we have included six special journal editions devoted to women students in higher education. These editions carry articles across a broad spectrum of interests, some of which are itemized in the entries.

Role Behavior

Athanassiades, J.C. The internalization of the female stereotype by college women. *Human Relations,* 1977, *30*(2), 187–199.

> The self concepts, public selves, and perceptions of the female stereotype of a sample of college women are examined. Results suggest that the female stereotype is not internalized but rather acts as an external behavioral constraint.

Baruch, G. Maternal influences upon college women's attitudes toward women and work. *Developmental Psychology,* 1972, *6*(1),32–37.

> From this study of 86 undergraduates, Baruch concluded that women tend to devalue female professional competence. Devaluation may result from an association of career and negative social consequences, or it may be an attitude learned from a non-working mother. The attitudes and experiences of maternal models with respect to work were relevant.

Coates, T. & Southern, M. Differential educational aspiration levels of men and women undergraduate students. *Journal of Psychology,* 1972, *81*(1), 125–128.

> This study of 198 male and 166 female undergraduates showed that significantly more males aspired to higher educational levels than did females. The lower aspiration of women may account, in part, for the underrepresentation of women in the professions.

Curtis, R.C., Zanna, M.P., & Campbell, W.W. Jr. Sex, fear of success, and the perceptions and performance of law school students. *American Educational Research Journal,* 1975, *12*(3), 287–297.

> This relatively small study found that fear of success and sex of respondent were independently associated with certain kinds of behavior among law students in the sample, but that there were no interaction effects. Women may be more likely than men to fear rejection, but they are not more likely to fear success.

Douvan, E. Higher education and feminine socialization. *New Directions for Higher Eduction,* 1975, *3*(1), 37–50.

> Presents the thesis that gender differences, whether physiological or learned, have implications for all aspects of life, including the ways in which people learn and the uses to which they put learning.

Epstein, G.F. & Bronzaft, A.L. Female freshmen view their roles as women. *Journal of Marriage and the Family,* November 1972, 671–672.

> Female students in this study, predominantly from lower middle-class and working-class backgrounds, saw their role fifteen years hence as "married career woman with children."

Gump, J.P. Comparative analysis of Black women's and White women's sex-role attitudes. *Journal of Consulting and Clinical Psychology,* 1975, *43*(6), 858–863.

> An assessment of the sex-role attitudes of 77 black college women and 40 White college women refuted the characterization of the Black women as matriarchal and the White women as home centered and submissive. Black women were more likely to define their identity with respect to the roles of wife and mother.

Gump, J.P. Sex-role attitudes and psychological well-being. *Journal of Social Issues,* 1972, *28(2),* 79–92.

> Gump found that the majority of 162 college senior women believed it possible to assume roles of wife and mother and to work. Neither happiness nor the establishment of relationships with men differentiated women with traditional sex-role orientations from those interested in realizing their own potentials. Students with the highest ego-strength were actively pursuing both marriage and careers.

Hall, D.T. A model of coping with role conflict: The role behavior of college-educated women. *Administrative Science Quarterly,* 1972, *17,* 471–486.

> Presents three general coping "types" into which 16 specific behavioral strategies identified in a survey of college-educated women are classified. The simple act of coping may be more closely related to satisfaction in women than the specific coping strategy employed. (Good bibliography on role conflict and coping with it.)

Horner, M.S. Women's will to fail. *Psychology Today,* March 1969, 36–38. (Based on the author's unpublished doctoral dissertation, University of Michigan, 1968.)

> The classic study of women's fear of success as a product of the socialization process. (A critique of Horner's research is provided by A. Tresemer who raises concerns about Horner's procedures and conclusions. Other studies have shown that men are also fearful of success. See: Tresemer, D. Fear of success: Popular but unproven. *Psychology Today,* 1974, *7*(10), 82–85.)

Huber, J. *Changing women in a changing society.* Chicago: University of Chicago Press, 1972.

> Huber's book considers: cultural contradications and sex roles, the success of black professional women, intellectual sexism, demographic influences on female employment, marriage and work, the woman's place in society.

Marecek, J. & Frasch, C. Locus of control and college women's role expectations. *Journal of Counseling Psychology,* 1977, *24*(2), 132–136.

> Research supporting the hypothesis that college women with an internal locus of control have higher aspirations, less conservative sex-role ideologies, and more involvement with career planning than women with an external locus of control.

Maxwell, P. & Gonzalez, C. Traditional and non-traditional role choice and need for failure among college women. *Psychological Reports,* 1972, *31*(1), 545–546.

>The authors studied 272 undergraduate females and found that a traditional role choice accompanied by a concomitant need for failure in domains of behavior defined as masculine.

Mednick, M.T.S. & Puryear, G.R. Race and fear of success in college women: 1968 and 1971. *Journal of Consulting and Clinical Psychology,* 1976, *44*(5), 787–789.

>The incidence of fear of success imagery was compared for Black and White women. Data collected in 1971 did not support the hypothesis of a race difference. This finding was in marked contrast to an earlier study of race differences in fear of success.

Oliver, L.W. The relationship of parental attidues and parent identification to career and homemaking orientation in college women. *Journal of Vocational Behavior,* 1975, 7(1), 1–11.

>The purpose of this research was to compare career oriented and homemaking oriented college women, who showed the motivational pattern previously found to be associated with their respective orientations, on the variables of parental attitudes (father and mother acceptance, concentration, and avoidance) and parent identification (father or mother).

Parelius, A.P. Emerging sex-role attitudes, expectations, and strains among college women. *Journal of Marriage and the Family,* 1975, *37*(1), 146–153.

>In this study a marked shift toward feminism was found in women's attitudes, but little change occured in their perception of men as relatively conservative. Strains may develop as more women adopt attitudes which they believe men reject.

Patty, R.A. *The motive to avoid success & instructional set.* Winston-Salem, North Carolina: Wake Forest University, Department of Psychology. Paper presented at the Annual Meeting of the American Psychological Association, New Orleans, Louisiana, August 1974.

>The motive to avoid success has been conceptualized as an ambivalence in life-goal directions, particularly characteristic of white college women. The presence or absence of the motive to avoid success was found to interact significantly with two experimental sets of instructions: difficult vs. easy (experiment 1) and internal vs. external (experiment 2) locus-of-control. Women exhibiting the motive to avoid success performed better on digit span

(backwards) following easy and external-control instructions while women not exhibiting the motive to avoid success performed better following difficult and internal-control instructions.

Rogers, J.C. *Role conflicts of college women,* 1976. [ERIC ED 126823]

> Forty-three female college students responded to a 15-statement questionnaire dealing with five areas of role conflict: (1) time management; (2) relations with spouse or boyfriend; (3) expectations for self; (4) expectations of others; and (5) guilt. The problem statements used in the questionnaire were derived from previous research that found "expectations for self" and "time management" to be the areas of greatest role conflict for women. For this sample, "expectations for self" was an area of little concern. Of more concern was the one area of guilt, focusing on the act of not doing what someone else wants done; essentially, a tendency to experience feelings of guilt following assertive behavior. "Time Management" was of concern but not to a significant degree.

Steinmann, A. Female role perception as a factor in counseling. *The Journal of the National Association for Women Deans, Administrators, and Counselors,* 1970, *34*(1), 27–33.

> Steinmann conducted a study to determine the basis for responses given by women on inventories of female values. A sample of college women (N=51) and their parents were interviewed. The author found that "the notions held by young women regarding work and family seem to reflect both the views and actions of their parents."

Streiker, A.B. & Johnson, J.E. Sex-role identification and self esteem in college students: Do men and women differ? *Sex Roles,* 1977, *3*(1), 19–26.

> In this study of 312 male and female college students, group self esteem scores did not differ significantly. The correlation of achievement motivation with self esteem was significant in both the male and female groups, but it was significantly stronger for females. A stereotypical masculine orientation was shown to have a direct relationship with self esteem in both males and females.

Travis, C.B. Women's liberation among two samples of young women. *Psychology of Women Quarterly,* 1976, *1*(2), 189–198.

> Interviews involving women university students in 1970 and 1971, revealed that the role of housewife and mother was idealized among those who were not participating in those roles.

Tresemer, D. Fear of success: Popular but unproven. *Psychology Today*, 1974, 7(10), 82–85.

> Refutes Horner's classic research on fear of success in women. Men have also demonstrated a fear of success in other studies.

Voss, J.H. & Skinner, D.A. Concepts of self and ideal woman held by college women: A replication. *Journal of College Student Personnel*, 1975, *16*(3), 210–213.

> Married and single female college students were compared in their perceptions of self, ideal woman, and man's ideal woman. Perceptions of female sex-role held by college women in 1969 and 1973 were also compared. Differences were found between the 1969 and 1973 groups.

Careers

Almquist, E.M. Sex stereotypes in occupational choice: The case for college women. *Journal of Vocational Behavior*, 1974, *5*, 13–21.

> The results of this longitudinal study indicate predictable differences between women choosing male-dominated occupations rather than traditionally feminine ones. The pattern of differences and similarities that was found precludes arguing that women choosing "male" occupations do so from social isolation, rejection, or lack of appropriate feminine socialization.

Almquist, E.M. & Angrist, S. Career salience and atypicality of occupational choice among college women. *Journal of the Marriage and the Family*, 1970, *32*, 242–248.

> Results of a four year longitudinal study of 110 students in a women's college within a coeducational university showed that "college graduate women who plan careers in occupational fields dominated by men are not necessarily different - in terms of dating, levels of participation in extracurricular activities, relationships to parents, and work values from non-career women who choose traditionally feminine occupations." The study suggests that a woman's career choice may be influenced by mother's work history, personal work experience, or role models.

Angrist, S. Variation in women's adult aspirations during college. *Journal of Marriage and the Family,* 1972, *34*, 465–468.

> A study conducted at Barnard showed five types of students. The "careerist" planned for both a family and an occupation, majored in the humanities, chose to pursue a male-dominated occupation, and was influenced by a working mother. She was not likely to belong to a sorority. The "convert" planned for both a family and an occupation by her senior year. The "noncareerist" was primarily oriented to a family role and was concerned with mate selection. The "defector" was career oriented as a freshman but family oriented by her senior year. The "shifter" changed goals frequently.

Astin, H.S. & Bisconti, A.S. *Trends in academic and career plans of college freshmen.* Bethlehem, PA: The CPC Foundation, Report No. 1, 1972.

> This monograph, the first of three, concluded that: women have generally aspired to lower career levels than men; majors in business and engineering attract a small proportion of women; fewer freshmen in 1970 than 1966 found "traditional life objectives" personally meaningful; men tended toward materialistic goals and goals of academic excellence while women tended toward altruistic goals.
> See also:
> — Report No. 2 in the same series entitled: *Career plans of college graduates of 1965 and 1970.*
> — Report No. 3 in the same series, entitled: *Career plans of Black and other non-White college graduates.*

Cherry, N. Occupational values and employment: A follow-up study of graduate men and women. *Higher Education,* 1975, *4*(3), 357–368.

> This study assesses whether the differences in undergraduate job values among men and women of varying social origins are of any occupational significance. The author concludes that graduates who held similar jobs at 26 years of age had similar job values at college. The need for a new approach to career education for the highly intelligent student of limited aspiration is emphasized. (Study was a sample of students (N=310) from throughout Great Britain.)

Edwards, J.N. & Klemmack, D.L. Birth order and the conservators of tradition hypothesis. *Journal of Marriage and the Family,* 1973, *35*(4), 619–625.

> An examination of the occupational aspirations held by 272 college women yielded limited support for the "conservators of tradition hypothesis" — the idea that first-born children are more likely to assume traditionally defined roles. Among women intending to enter the labor force, the first-born are more likely to aspire to traditionally non-feminine occupations.

Epstein, C.F. & Bronzaft, A.L. Female modesty in aspiration level. *Journal of Counseling Psychology,* 1974, *21*(1), 57–60.

> Highlights the need for women students and their counselors to match aspiration with ability, and to look beyond traditional "female" career tracks.

Farmer, H.S. & Bacher, T.E. *New career options for women. A counselors sourcebook.* New York: Human Sciences Press, 1977.

> A wealth of up-to-date information on women in the work force and on the educational and training opportunities available to women. Companion volume to the selected annotated bibliography of the same main title.

Harmon, L. Anatomy of career commitment in women. *Journal of Counseling Psychology,* 1970, *17*, 77–80.

> Ten to 14 years after college entrance, subjects were asked what their "usual career" was. Those who listed one were called "career committed"; those who listed none were called "noncommitted". Differences between the two groups were found, but none of them offered a basis for predicting career commitment before women begin programs of higher education.

Harmon, L. The childhood and adolescent career plans of college women. *Journal of Vocational Behavior,* 1971, *1*, 45–56.

> In 1968, 1188 freshman women were asked to report, retrospectively, which of 135 occupational titles they had ever considered as careers. A restricted range of occupations was considered early in life. While occupations preferred early were popular, not all early preferences persisted. Typically feminine occupations were the most persistent preferences of this group.

Herman, M.H. & Sedlacek, W.E. Career orientation of high school and university women. *The Journal of the National Association for Women Deans, Administrators, and Counselors,* 1974, *37*(4), 161–166.

> Career orientation of college women was studied through examiniation of type of major chosen and attitudes influencing career decisions. Subjects were senior university students. The study points out differences between women choosing occupations such as teaching and those choosing careers in science.

Hoffman, D. & Hoeflin, R. Freshman and sophmore women: What do they want most in the future? *Journal of College Student Personnel*, 1972, *13*(6), 490–493.

    The authors found that among 420 freshman and sophomore women, the majority of future plans included marriage and career.

Johnson, R.W. Parental identification and vocational interests of college women. *Measurement and Evaluation in Guidance*, 1970, *3*(3), 147–151.

    Career orientation in women does not necessarily represent identification with the male parent, or other cross-sex identification.

Karman, E.J. *Women: Personal and environmental factors in career choice* Presented at the Annual Meeting of the American Educational Research Association, New Orleans, Louisiana, February 25-March 1, 1973. [ERIC ED 074400]

    This study explores the psychological and sociological characteristics of two groups of women: those who choose careers in stereotypic masculine occupations versus those who select careers in stereotypic feminine fields such as teaching, nursing, social work, counseling, homemaking, library, and secretarial work. The sample consisted of 1646 upperclass college women of whom just 109 expressed career aspirations in nontraditional fields. Results suggest that women perceive a narrow range of career possibilities because they are fearful of venturing into a man's world; in addition, higher education has done little to expand women's awareness or interests beyond they sex stereotyped career roles. The author references other studies which indicate that counselors in higher education are ineffective in dealing with women students who are considering male-dominated careers. References are included.

Luria, Z. Recent women college graduates: A study of rising expectations. *American Journal of Orthopsychiatry*, 1974, *44*, 312–326.

    A sample of 1969 and 1970 women college graduates differs significantly from a similar sample in 1967 and 1968 in having higher motivation to work, especially when the youngest child is 2 to 6 years old. Marriage does not play the critical role in career planning among the more recent group that it plays for the 1967 and 1968 graduates. (Author's abstract)

McMillan, M.R., Cerra, P.F., & McHaffey, T.D. Opinions on career involvement of married women. *The Journal of the National Association for Women Deans, Administrators, and Counselors*, 1971, *34*(3), 121–124.

    The results of this study show that a potential area of conflict exists for young adults regarding the career involvement of the wife. College women preferred a career and marriage rather than either alone, while college men preferred that their wives not work after the birth of children.

McMillan, M.R. Vocational commitment of college women. *The Journal of the National Association for Women Deans, Administrators, and Counselors*, 1974, *37*(4), 158–160.

Assesses the vocational commitment of college women who have spent time, energy and money preparing for a profession. Subjects were senior undergraduate women from a large southern university. Results indicated women desired active involvement in their profession.

Moore, K.M. & Veres, H.C. Traditional and innovative career plans of two-year college women. *Journal of College Student Personnel*, 1976, *17*(1), 34–38.

Differences between groups of women in two-year colleges who are planning traditional and innovative careers and lifestyles are discussed, with emphasis on the implications for counselors. Each group reveals unique perceptions and needs as students and as women. Counselors are urged to develop ways to help both groups of women students.

Notestine, E.B. & Kerlin, L. A look at recent college graduates. *Vocational Guidance Quarterly*, 1975, *24*(1), 56–61.

This study compared the salaries of 1968 men and women college graduates at the time of their first salary level and current salary level; it also compares the lowest and highest initial offers among the two groups. The authors found that there is substance to the claim of salary discrimination against women college graduates.

Parrish, J.B. Women, careers and counseling: The new era. *The Journal of the National Association for Women Deans, Administrators, and Counselors*, 1974, *37*(1),11–19.

Discusses the prospects for women with college degrees vis-a-vis new labor market conditions in the 1970's. Eight major characteristics of the market are noted, with implications for college-educated women. Finally, the task ahead for counselors is outlined.

Phelps, A.T., Farmer, H.S. & Bacher, T.E. *New career options for women. A selected annotated bibliography.* New York: Human Sciences Press, 1977.

Covers research and related works, mostly since 1970, on the following topics: 1) career opportunities for women particularly in occupations formerly dominated by men, 2) legal rights of women relative to work, 3) counseling techniques and strategies, 4) current social science research on women in the work force. See especially section III (p. 47) on "women's opportunities in training and education." Companion volume to the counselor's sourcebook of the same main title.

Richardson, M.S. Self-concepts and role concepts in the orientation of college women. *Journal of Counseling Psychology,* 1975, *22*(2), 122–126.

This study examined the relationship between nine career orientation variables and 97 college women's self concepts and role concepts. Results supported the expectation that women with self- and role concepts related to homemaking would not be career oriented.

Richardson, M.S. The dimensions of career and work orientation in college women. *Journal of Vocational Behavior,* 1974, *5*(1), 161–172.

Fourteen presumed measures of career orientation as well as Super's work values inventory were administered to college women. Work-oriented women tended to choose traditionally feminine occupations in contrast to the career-oriented women whose aspirations included higher level and less traditional occupations.

Richardson, M.S. and others. Vocational maturity and career orientation in college women. Paper presented at the Eastern Psychological Association, New York, N.Y. April 22–24, 1976 [ERIC ED 134911].

Two studies, the second essentially a replication of the first, were conducted to clarify the meaning of vocational maturity in female career development. While no significant relationship between career orientation variables and vocational maturity was obtained in the first study, work role salience was positively related to vocational maturity in the second study. Correlation matrices of the career orientation variables in both studies revealed that the two dimensions of career orientation are independent in college women. Results are discussed in the context of Crites' theoretical model of vocational maturity and current expectations for female career participation. Implications for further research in female career development are presented.

Rose, H. & Elton, C. Sex and occupational choice. *Journal of Counseling Psychology,* 1971, *18*, 456–461.

This is the presentation of a study of Omnibus Personality Scores of males and females graduating in majors classified into five Holland occupational categories. The authors concluded that separate theories of occupational choice are necessary if the theories are to be based on vocational constructs.

Sherman, R.G. & Jones, J.H. Career choices for women - new determinants. *Journal of College Student Personnel,* 1976, *17*(4), 289–294.

> Career choices for college women now depend upon different factors from those in the past. The new determinants have relevance for counselors and other college professionals. Despite contrary pressures, women are moving in the direction of economic independence and a high level of professional aspiration.

Tangri, S.S. Determinants of occupational role innovation among college women. *Journal of Social Issues,* 1972, *28*(2), 177–200.

> This study of 200 senior college women investigates the relationship between non-sextypical occupational choices (role innovation) and background, personality, and college experience.

Trigg, L.J. & Perlman, D. Social influences on women's pursuit of a non-traditional career. *Psychology of Women Quarterly,* 1976, *1*(2), 138–149.

> Three hypotheses were derived from the basic premise that, among women, social factors are crucial in the choice of a high status, nontraditional career. All three hypotheses were supported in a questionnaire study of 153 nursing and medical rehabilitation applicants (traditional) versus 78 medical and dental applicants (non-traditional).

Turner, B.F. & McCaffrey, J.H. Socialization and career orientation among Black and White college women. *Journal of Vocationsl Behavior,* 1974, *5*(3), 307–319.

> In a study of career orientation among black and white college women, support was found for hypotheses derived from Rotter's social learning theory. As hypothesized, variables expressive of external control predicted level of career expectation among blacks, whereas variables expressive of internal control predicted high career expectations among whites. [Small samples are used only, and the white sample is not representative. The authors indicate these limitations and offer their findings as "tentative."]

Valentine, D., Ellinger, N., & William, M. Sex-role attributes and career choice of male and female graduate students. *Vocational Guidance Quarterly,* 1975, *24*(1), 48–53.

> This study concludes that graduate students, both men and women, who choose professions generally thought to be appropriate for the opposite sex are more liberal in their attitudes toward women's roles than students choosing same-sex professions.

Veres, H.C. *Career choice and career commitment of two-year college women.* Paper presented at the 59th Annual Meeting of the American Educational Research Association, Chicago, Illinois, April 1974 [ERIC ED 091020].

The influence of the mother over daughter's career commitment and perceptions of appropriate occupational choices were studied in a random sample of students in a two-year comprehensive community college. Results of the study showed that no relationship existed between the work history of the mother and the career choice of the subject. The mothers of the group were typically employed in office work or in occupations relating to housekeeping skills and/or child care. The dimension of career commitment yielded significant positive relationships with the length of time the subject's mother had been employed and whether she was presently working. These observations tend to support a modeling influence of mother upon daughter. It is concluded that young women need exposure to a wider variety of role-models, as well as increased information, support, and encouragement from faculty and counselors concerning entrance into non-traditional occupational areas.

Wolfson, K.P. Career development patterns of college women. *Journal of Counseling Psychology,* 1976, *23*(2), 119–125.

Women who had been college students in the mid-thirties (N=306) and who had been studied 25 years later were assigned to five vocational pattern groups. A woman's career pattern could not be predicted from data available at the time she entered college, but was predictable from other data known five years later.

College/Student Interactions

Bertelson, J. *Two studies of women in higher education.* Oakland, CA: Mills College (mimeo), 1974.

I. Impact of coeducation on colleges previously for women only

The first study begins with a discussion of the terms "coeducation" and "singlesex" applied to higher education, and then examines four propositions concerning co-education on the basis of existing research conducted by single-sexinstitutions. Short run impacts and long-range prospects are discussed.

II. Women's center survey

The second piece reports results of a questionnaire survey of all known women's centers on U.S. college campuses.

Brush, L.R. Choosing a women's college. *College and University,* 1976, *51*(3), 360–67.

> A comparative study of women at three women's colleges and one coeducational college showed major reasons for college choice to be academic criteria, institutional characteristics, school size, and social factors. Compared to students in a 1958 study, contemporary students emphasized social features and deemphasized personal values and the advice of others.

Conway, J. & Jordan, P. Are women's colleges necessary today? *The New York Times.* November 13, 1977, p. Education Section 13.

> Two college presidents argue the cases for and against women's colleges, Conway arguing that they teach self-confidence and Jordan arguing that they foster isolation.

Dickerson, K. Are female college students influenced by the expectations they perceive their faculties and administrators to have for them? *The Journal of the National Association for Women Deans, Administrators, and Counselors,* 1974, *37*, 167–172.

> Dickerson found that if a women feels that faculty and administration have high expectations for her, her own aspirations are raised. Conversely, low expectations may result in low aspirations.

Etaugh, C. & Bowen, L. Attitudes toward women: Comparison of enrolled and non-enrolled college students. *Psychological Reports,* 1976, *38*,(1), 229–230.

> Data from this study suggest that the more liberal attitudes generally associated with progress through the college years may be partly due to the dropout of traditionally-minded women; enrolled women were more liberal than non-enrolled women whereas the converse was true for men.

Farley, J. Coeducation and college women. *The Cornell Journal of Social Relations,* 1974, *9*(1), 87–97.

> This study of 1870 Cornell undergraduates suggested that even women in an institution that has been coeducational since 1874 still choose a more limited range of fields than their male classmates, despite achievement of higher grades than their male counterparts. An expansion of women's perception of their own capabilities is called for, as well as an equalization of opportunities.

Gillie, A. *The differential effects of selected programs on the performance, degree of satisfaction, and retention of community college women students. Final Report.* The Pennsylvania State University, October 1972.

> Gillie studied female postsecondary students to discover how they viewed themselves within the college environment. One of the few studies that focuses on women in community colleges.

Husbands, S. Women's place in higher education. *School Review,* 1972, *80,* 261–274.

> Factors in the college environment most likely to affect women's aspirations are relationships with peers and faculty, sex composition of students, and curricula offerings of the school.

Keller, B.B. & Chambers, J.L. Motivation factors in organized student group participation. *Journal of College Student Personnel,* 1975, *16*(4), 313–315.

> Picture idenitification test scores of 188 college women who participated in several extracurricular activities were compared with those who participated less. Results suggested that women who took part in no activities were more concerned about avoiding failure than more active women, and preferred to stay out of extracurricular activities.

Leland, C.A. & Lozoff, M.M. *College influences on the role development of female undergraduates.* Stanford CA: Stanford University, 1969. [ERIC ED 026975]

> This study investigates psychosocial factors affecting the education and occupational development of female undergraduates. The first part comprises an extensive literature review, and the second part is the analysis of longitudinal data from a four year study. Autonomy achieved by college women is influenced by background factors — parental influences in particular — and predicts life style in and after college.

Lester, D. & Lester, G. Preliminary note on a search for correlates of attitudes toward coeducation from female college students. *Psychological Reports,* 1974, *35*(1), 10–10.

> Few women in two small questionnaire surveys at Wheaton College and Wellesly College appeared to desire isolation at a women's college. Some form of coeducation or merger was the majority wish.

McCarty, P. A new perspective on women's colleges. *The Journal of the National Association for Women Deans, Administrators, and Counselors,* 1977, *40*(1), 65–67.

> Pros and cons of attending a women's college. (Not research, but well-reasoned.)

Moore, K.M. The cooling out of two-year college women. *Personnel & Guidance Journal,* 1975, *53*(8), 578–583.

> The author describes the concept of "cooling out" as developed by Burton Clark and examines its applicability to the experience of women in the two-year college. The author concludes that cooling out as experienced by women is congruent with but not exactly like the process as described by Clark.

Patterson, M. *The impact of colleges and universities on the educational aspirations of women.* Final Report. Santa Barbara, CA: University of California, 1976. [ERIC ED 136645].

> This study examines the way in which institutions of higher education change or fail to change the educational aspirations of women students. Variations in aspiration that were present after one year had washed out by the fourth year in college.

Schmidt, M.R. Personality change in college women. *Journal of College Student Personnel,* 1970, *11*(6), 414–418.

> Females entering as freshmen at the University of Iowa were tested during orientation and again as seniors. Results indicate a decrease in dogmatism, increase in interpersonal competence, and an increase in selectivity regarding preferred occupations.

Seltzer, M.M. Contemporary college women view their roles. *Journal of College Student Personnel,* 1975, *16*(4), 265–269.

> Analysis of responses to a series of stories obtained from a sample of midwestern college women showed that freshmen women were more traditional and less secular in orientation toward the role of women than were upperclass and PhD. students.

Sternglanz, S.H. & Lyberger-Ficek, S. Sex differences in student-teacher interactions in the college classroom. *Sex Roles,* 1977, *3*(4), 345–352.

> Male and female students and professors were observed in 60 college classes. In classes taught by males, males were more numerous and dominated

student-teacher interactions; in class taught by females there were no sex differences in these measures.

Tidball, M.E. On liberation and competence. *Educational Record,* 1976, *57*(2), 101–110.

Educators need to do more thinking about the environment they create for students, and for women students in particular. The author intends to encourage thinking and discussion on how best to deliberately and positively promote the maximum unhomogenized development of both young women and young men.

Tidball, M.E. The search for talented women. *Change,* 1974, *6*(4), 41–52,64.

Successful women professionals have two characteristics in common: they are graduates of women's colleges and unmarried. The author concludes that coeducational colleges are preoccupied with the needs of their men students and have virtually ignored the needs of women.

Weston, L.C. & Stein, S.L. The relationship of the identity achievement of college women and campus participation. *Journal of College Student Personnel,* 1977, *18*(1), 21–24.

The relationship between participation in campus organizations and identity achievement is investigated. A study involving approximately 300 college women at a four-year, private, Eastern secular college revealed that degree of activity was related to identity achievement. A test of the relationship between type of housing and campus participation supported previous findings.

Adult Women in Higher Education

Astin, H.S. (Ed.) *Some action of her own: The adult woman and higher education.* Lexington, MA: D.C. Heath and Co., 1976.

"This book was designed to give an analytic account of the development of programs of continuing education for women (CEW), of the impact of these programs in the lives of the women they serve, and their influence in the institutions which house them and in higher education in general." (p. vii)

Brandenburg, J.B. The needs of women returning to school. *Personnel and Guidance Journal,* 1974, *53*(1), 11–18.

A position paper dealing with the needs of mature women matriculants, and how those needs might be met.

Cross, K.P. Women as new students. In K.P. Cross, *Beyond the Open Door*, San Francisco: Jossey-Bass, 1971.

"New students" in higher education will include more women than ever, and this chapter provides a research description of the female "new student" contingent.

de Wolf, V. & Lunneborg, P.W. *Descriptive information on over-35 undergraduate students*. Seattle, WA: University of Washington Bureau of Testing, 1972. [ERIC ED 072745].

This report summarizes information about the 100 women and 53 men over 35 years of age who entered the University of Washington as undergraduates between spring 1970 and autumn 1971. The information was provided by the participants on a biographic survey that was administered at the same time as the Washington Pre-College Test Battery. High school background and early family life, prior education and vocational/educational goals, community and employment activities are covered in addition to current major, class, and academic status. Attention is directed throughout to differences between the sexes of which the most noteworthy findings appear to be the higher secondary school performance and lower aspirations of the females in the sample.

Durcholz, P. & O'Connor, J. Why women go back to college. *Change*, 1973, 5(8), 52 & 62.

A survey of the reasons women over 25 returned to college, their aspirations, and the barriers affecting them.

Geisler, M.P. & Thrush, R.S. Counseling experiences & needs of older women students. 1975, *The Journal of the National Association for Women Deans, Administrators, and Counselors*, 1975, 39(1), 3–7.

Report of a study of women aged 28 and older (N=264) at a large public university to determine their counseling needs and experiences. Expressed needs included vocational, educational, personal, and financial counseling; also included were assistance with study skills and credit for life experience. Problem areas were role definition, self-confidence, sense of direction, child care and course scheduling. (Good list of references on adult students in academe.)

Hull, D. *Maturity as a variable in predicting academic success*. Columbia, Missouri: University of Missouri, 1970. [ERIC ED 045039].

This study sought to determine whether maturity contributes to academic success, and therefore whether it should be taken into consideration in the admission of students. The results suggest that maturity positively affects academic success as measured by grade point averages.

Katz, J. and others. *Educational and occupational aspirations of adult women. Report to the College Entrance Examination Board.* Stanford CA: Stanford Institute for Study of Human Problems, 1970. [ERIC ED 045005].

The first chapter of this report, "Career and autonomy in college women," deals with the career choice of undergraduate women at San Jose City College and Stanford University. Chapter 2, "Adult women at work and at home" and Chapter 3, "Career-oriented versus home-oriented women," present data based on 1) questionnaire responses from alumnae of Santa Rosa Junior College and Stanford University who were between 26 and 50 years old in 1968; 2) hour-by-hour diaries of ten full days in the lives of seventeen college educated adult women in the San Francisco peninsula area, and from interviews with 27 of the women who had completed the questionnaires. Chapter 4, "Images of women in women's magazines," presents a content analysis of a selected number of women's magazines in terms of the attitudes towards education, career, and home that are held or presumably held, by middle-class adult women. Chapter 5, "Selected bibliography on women: 1950–1969," presents a survey of an annotated bibliography of the literature on the educational and occupational situation of adult women.

Mulligan, K.L. *A question of opportunity: Women and continuing education.* Washington D.C.: National Advisory Council on Extension and Continuing Education, March 1973. [ERIC ED 081323].

This document examines the issue of women and continuing education. Part one reviews the relevant research concerning employment, traditional university offerings, and vocational and educational lifestyles of women. Part two describes the results of a questionnaire sent to 376 program directors in an attempt to learn priorities for federal funds and something about the more successful models of programs for women. A review of educational legislation revealed that there are provisions that would permit the funding of services and/or research that would promote more effective development of programs for women. Part three assesses the impact of these activities and identifies potential funding sources for practitioners in the field.

Nichols, C.G. A seminar in personality development for mature women. *The Journal of the National Association for Women Deans, Administrators, and Counselors,* 1974, *38*(3), 123–127.

Nichols assessed the effects of a special one-semester seminar intended to help mature women who wish to re-enter academe make the transition. Participation in the seminar was considered helpful.

O'Connell, A.N. The decision to return to college: Role concepts, personality, attitudes and significant others. *Sex Roles,* 1977, *3*(3), 229–240.

"In two studies, personality, role concepts, and attitudes distinguished wives and mothers who decided to resume college from those who did not. College women and women about to resume college had: personalities that were more self-actualizing, achievement-oriented, and dominant; broader more personalized role concepts; more liberated attitudes; better educated husbands; and fewer children than housewives. Measurements before college return and during the second year at college indicated that college exposure did not significantly affect these variables. The single exception was that after exposure to college women no longer saw society as supporting their efforts to actualize their potentials." (Edited article abstract.)

Rice, J.K. & Goering, M.C. Women in transition: A life-planning workshop model. *The Journal of the National Association for Women Deans, Administrators, and Counselors,* 1977, *40*(1), 57–61.

This study assessed a workshop approach to providing returning women students with transition from home to school or work. The authors conclude that a "simple in-depth workshop experience can be quite effective in facilitating planning and decision-making of returning adults."

Tittle, C.K. & Denker, E.R. Re-entry women: A selective review of the educational process, career choice, and interest measurement. *Review of Educational Research,* 1977, *47*(4), 531–584.

The review covers: a) barriers and opportunities for the re-entry woman in higher education, b) current theory and research on career choice for women, c) interest inventories as a counseling tool for reentry women. It is a rich source of information on these issues, both as a review of the literature and as an interpretation of its implications for further work in this field.

Wells, J.A. *Continuing education for women: current developments.* Washington, D.C.: Women's Bureau, 1974.

A valuable source of current factual material to anyone involved in research in the women's continuing education field.

Wilms, B. Getting at the women's market in higher education. *College Management,* 1973, *8*(7), 32–33.

The Center for the Continuing Education of Women at the University of California Berkeley is presented in this article as a workable approach for getting women back into the mainstream of higher education as well as into the job they want.

Discrimination

Bengelsdorf, W. *Women's stake in low tuition.* Washington, D.C.: American Association of State Colleges and Universities, 1974. [ERIC ED 096933].

This pamphlet focuses on women's stake in low tuition. Eight key points are suggested: (1) a much smaller percentage of qualified women than men attend college; (2) women from low-income and minority families have less chance for college; (3) women get less student financial aid than men; (4) women in college have fewer work-study opportunities; (5) parttime and older women as well as men are discriminated against; (6) older women have much lower incomes than men and cannot afford high college costs; (7) long-term loan plans discriminate against women even more than men; (8) low tuition public higher education is as essential for women as it is for many other minorities, families in rural and small town areas, businessmen, and American society as a whole.

Boulding, E. The global macroproblem: Prospects for women and minorities. *Liberal Education,* 1976, *62*(2), 185–207.

A serious obstacle to releasing the creativity of minority groups for future problem solving is the attitude of white middle-class males, particularly in colleges and universities, who think they are advancing the cause of minorities when they are not. Advances made by minorities are reviewed, along with their resources and some recommendations to college administrators.

Chobot, D.S., Goldberg, P.A. Abramson, L.M. & Abramson, P.R. Prejudice against women: A replication and extension. *Psychological Reports,* 1974, *35*(1), 478.

This study refutes Goldberg's findings that women are prejudiced against professional women. In this research, neither male nor female college students rated articles said to be written by men higher than the same articles said to be written by women.

Ekstrom, R.B. *Barriers to women's participation in post-secondary education. A review of the literature.* Princeton, N.J.: Educational Testing Service, October 1972. [ERIC ED 072368].

Although the phenomenon has long been observed that women enter all types of post-secondary education at lower participation rates than men, there have been few attempts to analyze the reasons for this. These barriers may be categorized as (1) institutional, (2) situational, and (3) dispositional. Institutional factors that serve to exclude women from participation in post-secondary education include admissions practices, financial aid practices, institutional regulations, types of curriculum and services adopted, and faculty and staff attitudes. Situational barriers that deter women from participation in further education include family responsibilities, financial need, and societal pressures. Dispositional barriers that prevent women from continuing education include their fear of failure, attitude toward intellectual activity, role preference, ambivalence about educational goals, level of aspiration, passivity, dependence, and inferiority feelings. References are included. (Author's abstract)

Ewald, L.S. Sex discrimination in higher education: Constitutional equality for women? *Journal of Family Law,* 1971, *10*, 327–343.

A discussion of four cases involving sex discrimination in admissions procedures; the reasonings decisions, and implications of the courts' actions on achieving equal education opportunities are presented.

Fitzpatrick, B. *Women's inferior education.* New York: Praeger, 1976.

Analyzes options available to young women after high school, in academic and vocational education, in the U.S. and in each of 20 states. Documents discriminatory use of state and federal tax revenue to support the postsecondary education of many more men than women. Uses economic theory to explain discrimination by decision makers in education. Recommends action by young women, their parents and tax-payers to assure equal opportunity for the equally qualified.

Groszko, M. & Morgenstern, R. Institutional discrimination: the case of achievement oriented women in higher education. *International Journal of Group Tensions,* 1974, *4*(1) 82–92.

This study, like others, shows that institutions of higher education practice systematic discrimination against women in the sense that they "inculcate and reinforce personality characteristics consistent with the feminine stereotype (in need achievement and fear of success) and fail to encourage those traits which allow one to become a competent and efficient achiever.
N.B.: This entire issue (Florence Denmark, Ed) treats the subject of sex-based discrimination.

Leslie, L.L. *Higher education opportunity: A decade of progress.* Washington, D.C.: AAHE/ERIC Research Report No. 3, 1977.

The section of this monograph entitled "Enrollment trends by sex" (pp. 39–42) provides several pertinent analyses and conclusions. Among them:
— women are increasing their enrollment share, but remain under-represented.

— fewer women than men are breaking tradition and enrolling for the first time.
— women corner slightly more of the financial aid market than men, but would attend college and cover own expenses regardless, unlike men.
— women are: underrepresented in private universities, overrepresented in four year colleges (private and public) equally represented in universities overall, and most conspicuously underrepresented in upper level institutions.
— women pay less than men to attend college because they receive more financial aid.

McBee, M.L. & Suddick, D.E. Differential freshman admission by sex. *The Journal of the National Association for Women Deans, Administrators, and Counselors*, 1974, *37*(2), 75–78.

The authors use a statistical model to determine whether differential admissions criteria by sex were justifiable after adjusting for implicit differences (high school grade point average, and SAT scores). They conclude that the use of differential cutoff scores in a quota system is unwarranted.

Magarrell, J. Women account for 93 percent of enrollment gain. *The Chronicle of Higher Education*, 1978, *15*(7), pp. 1,9.

Statistical report on the growth in numbers of female students in the 1976–1977 academic year. Women now account for 49% of the total U.S. college enrollment.

Mickelson, S. *Women graduates. A statistical survey of the proportion of women earning degrees in higher education in the United States. A Weal Fund report for International Woman's Year.* Washington, D.C.: Women's Equity Action League, 1975. [ERIC ED 116517].

In 1971, the Council for University Women's Progress first prepared tables which compared all Ph.D's attained by women to those attained by men in the same fields. The present document brings this data up to date and supplements it with tables on Master's and Bachelor's degrees, as well as first professional degrees. The tables show data such as the proportion of Bachelor's, Master's and doctoral degrees earned by women by major field of study and selected subfield; the proportion of first professional degrees earned by women; Bachelor's, Master's and doctorates earned by women by major field and as a percentage of all degrees earned by women for the periods 1960–1961 and 1971–1972. These data have supplied some evidence that women's career interests are changing.

Occhionero, M.F. La partecipazione femminile nell' universitaca Italiana. *Sociologia,* 1975, *9*(3), 59–75.

>The strong discrimination against coeducation in Italian universitites is documented as intrinsic to the chauvinistically male institution.

Sewell, W.H. Inequality of opportunity for higher education. *American Sociological Review,* 1971, *36*(5), 793–809.

>Women are most seriously disadvantaged by comparison to men in encouragement from parents and teachers, and in their own level of aspiration. (Also deals with effects of SES, race, and ethnic background.)

Wild, C.L. Statistical issues raised by Title IX requirements on admissions procedures. *The Journal of the National Association for Women Deans, Administrators, and Counselors,* 1977, *40(1), 53–56.*

>Shows that admission procedures treating males and females identicially may be unfair to female applicants.

Zell, L.C. & Weld, E.A., Jr. *Women's participation in higher education: A case study of degrees conferred by field of study by nine colleges and universities in the Cleveland metropolitan area, 1973–1974.* Cleveland, OH: Cleveland State University, Institute of Urban Studies, 1974.

>The study examines the kinds of education and training that women have been receiving from institutions of higher education in the Cleveland area and particularly in Cuyahoga County. Records of degrees conferred in 1973–1974 by program of study were secured from nine colleges and universities in Cuyahoga County (Baldwin-Wallace, Case Western Reserve University, Cleveland State University, Cuyahoga Community College, Dyke, John Carrol University, Notre Dame, St. John College, and Ursuline College) with total enrollments of 52,855. The percentage distribution of degrees granted per 100,000 population are compared with national average figures (1970–1971) from the Department of Health, Education, and Welfare. The survey data showed that most women receiving degrees in Cuyahoga County have been trained in traditionally 'female' fields of specialization; few women have received degrees in traditionally 'male' fields; and the absence of women in education and training programs leading to male occupations is true of all types of postsecondary education and training. The report further discusses possible factors accounting for the small number of women in traditionally 'male' programs of study. The study concludes with a list of priority areas for further investigation.

Alper, T.G. Achievement motivation in college women: A now-you-see-it-now-you-don't phenomenon. *American Psychologist,* 1970, *29*(3), 194–203.

> Examines the differences between females and males in academic motivation and concludes that previous attitudes toward achievement may be changing.

Bailey, R.C., Zinser, O., & Edgar, R. Perceived intelligence, motivation, and achievement in male and female college students. *Journal of Genetic Psychology,* 1975, *127*(1), 125–129.

> Males and females in this study regarded the typical female student as more intelligent, more motivated and more academically sucessful than the typical male student. Males and females regarded their intelligence similarly, but women saw themselves as having higher motivation and achievement than males.

Gadzella, B.M. & Fournet, G.P. Sex differences in self-perceptions as students of excellence and academic performance. *Perceptual and Motor Skills,* 1976, *43*(3), 1092–1094.

> The findings of this study show that female students rate themselves significantly higher than men on learning in class, study habits, and attitudes and peer relationships. Females also perceive upward changes in these areas over the semester and do better on measures of academic performance.

Harmon, L. Variables related to women's persistence in educational plans. *Journal of Vocational Behavior,* 1972, *2*, 143–153.

> This follow up study of female students in schools of nursing, medical technology, and social work showed that persistence was significantly related to birth order and mother's lifestyle.

Heilbrun, A.B., Jr. Developmental and situational correlates of achievement behavior in college females. *Journal of Personality,* 1974, *42*, 420–436.

> The explanation of achievement is far more complicated in the case of women than men. Women who do achieve generally perceive themselves to be more like their father than their mother. In this latter group, two further role-achievement patterns are identified and discussed.

Hewitt, B.N. & Goldman, R.D. Occam's razor slices through the myth that college women overachieve. *Journal of Educational Psychology*, 1975, 67(2), 325–330.

> Uses semi-partial correlation to show that almost all of the "overachievement" of women college students as opposed to men is accounted for by controlling for major field. (Women are clustered in fields where grading is more lenient.)

Horner, M. Toward an understanding of achievement-related conflicts in women. *Journal of Social Issues*, 1972, 25(2), 159–176.

> Horner looked at the motive to avoid success within the framework of the expectancy-value theory of motivation. She found that the expectation that success in achievement related situations would be followed by negative consequences aroused fear of success in otherwise achievement-motivated women. Their performances were, then, inhibited. Horner says that competence, independence, competition, and intellectual achievement are viewed as qualities basically inconsistent with femininity.

Oliver, L.W. Achievement and affiliation motivation in career-oriented and homemaking-oriented college women. *Journal of Vocational Behavior*, 1974, 4(3), 275–280.

> The purpose of this research was to investigate the possibility of an interaction between need for achievement and need for affiliation in career-oriented and homemaking-oriented college women. As predicted, a significant interaction occurred between the two variables.

Smith, D.G. Personality differences between persisters and withdrawers in a small women's college. *Research in Higher Education*, 1976, 5(1), 15–25.

> Differential effects of a particular small women's college environment on the attrition of its students were studied in two separate entering classes. The study supports the thesis that important personality characteristics discriminate between persisters and withdrawers.

Ten Elshof, A. & Mehl, D. *Academic achievement in college women. The Journal of the National Association for Women Deans, Administrators, and Counselors*, 1976, 40(1), 7–10.

> A study of parental influence on motivation of college women. Their general conclusion is that "freedom from a prescribed sex role definition had a positive effect on the academic achievement of women in the study."

Alperson, E.D. The minority woman in academe. *Professional Psychologist,* 1975, 6(3), 252–256.

> Deals with minorities and minority women's position vis a vis hiring practices, and subsequent expectations of academic institutions. Special attention is paid to departments of psychology.

Littig, L.W. *A study of certain personality correlates of occupational aspirations of Black and White college women.* Final Report. Washington, D.C.: Howard University, Department of Psychology, 1971.

> As part of a series of studies investigating occupational aspirations, this study explores the relationships between certain types of motivation and the occupational aspirations of Black and White female college students. With emphasis on occupations which, by tradition, have been either open or closed to Blacks, the design of the study involved three samples of 100 college women from three social settings — white middle class, black middle class, and Black working class. The data revealed no systematic relationships between motivation indices and aspiration to the above occupations. However, it was noted that Whites were more indecisive than Blacks regarding their real occupational goals and their ideal occupational goals. Further it is suggested that Black women are more career-oriented and use the same occupations when responding to questions about their ideal goal as they do when stating their real goal.

Minority Women and Higher Education, No. 1. Washington, D.C.: Association of American Colleges, Project on the Status and Education of Women, 1974.

> Various myths concerning black women and their educational status are examined, with current statistics provided to indicate their validity. Overall results of this examination indicate that minority women fare less well than minority men, just as white women fare less well than white men. It is suggested that minority women are affected by both sex and race discrimination and that they will not have a fair economic or educational opportunity unless and until both types of discrimination are eliminated. Just as efforts to remove racial barriers help minority women as well as minority men, efforts to remove sex barriers benefit minority women as well as white women.

Puryear, G.R. & Mednick, M.S. Black militancy, affective attachment, and the fear of success in Black college women. *Journal of Consulting and Clinical Psychology,* 1974, 42(2), 263–266.

> An examination of fear of success in Black college women at four campuses

indicates that the proportion of fear of success found in thematic apperception test imagery of Black women is consistently lower than has been found in studies of such imagery of White women.

Recruiting Minority Women, No. 2. Washington, D.C.: Association of American Colleges, Project on the Status and Education of Women, 1974.

The number of special resources for recruiting minority women is slowly increasing, although still limited. This document lists studies and handbooks, directories, registries and placement agencies, national organizations and women's groups, publications and directories of other media.

Weston, P.J. & Mednick, M.T. Race, social class and the motive to avoid success in women. *Journal of Cross Cultural Psychology,* 1970, *1*(3), 283–291.

Examines race and social class differences in the expression of fear of success (termed M-S) in college women. The hypothesis that Black women would show less M-S than white women was supported. Social class differences were not found. [Based on senior author's M.A. thesis in psychology at Howard University.]

Characteristics of Women Students

Cope, R.G. Sex-related factors and attrition among college women. *The Journal of the National Association for Women Deans, Administrators, and Counselors,* 1970, *33*(3), 118–124.

Reports the results of a study at the University of Massachusetts intended to compare female and male persistence in college on the basis of certain social and psychological criteria. Persistence among women was linked to esthetic inclination, physical attractiveness, and verbal aptitude.

Cross, K.P. College women: A research description. *The Journal of the National Association for Women Deans, Administrators, and Counselors,* 1968, *32(1), 12–21.*

A synthesis of research conducted in the 1960's on college students yields interesting differences between college men and women in background, attitudes, and aspirations. Recommendations on how to render higher education adequately flexible to accomodate the needs of women are offered.

Cross, K.P. *The undergraduate woman.* Washington, D.C.: American Association for Higher Education - Research Report, 1971.

> This report summarizes research on the undergraduate woman and discusses women as students, women's career aspirations, and the changing attitudes of women undergraduates toward their future roles.

Gearty, J.Z. & Milner, J.S. Academic major, gender of examiner, and motive to avoid success in women. *Journal of Clinical Psychology,* 1975, *31*(1), 13–14.

> This is basically a replication and extension of Horner's (1968) doctoral dissertation on female motive to avoid success, [Sex differences in achievement motivation and performance in competitive and non-competitive situations. University of Michigan, Ann Arbor, University Microfilms, 1968, No. 69–12, 135.] The authors found that the motive to avoid success was prevalent in their sample, and suggest that it is prevalent among female undergraduates as a whole.

Glass, K.D. & Schoch, E.W. Religious belief and practice related to anxiety and dogmatism in college women. *The Journal of the National Association for Women Deans, Administrators, and Counselors*, 1971, *34*(3), 130–133.

> Using a large sample of college freshmen and sophomore females (N=495) and four standardized instruments measuring religious belief, religious practice, anxiety, and dogmatism, the authors found that "the individual who practices his religion regularly emerged as the person most likely to avoid the dogmatism associated with the high belief but low practice individual and is likely to be more secure than the person who does not practice his religion consistently."

Faunce, P.S. & Loper, R.G. Personality characteristics of high anxiety college women and college women in general. *Journal of College Student Personnel*, 1972, *13*(6), 499–504.

> Differences in personality characteristics seem to exist between high ability freshman women and freshman women in general. Counselors, educators, and administrators should be aware of these differences and should not automatically assume similarity in personality characteristics among college women.

Moore, K.M. & Veres, H.C. *A study of two-year college women in central New York state: Characteristics, career determinants and perceptions.* New York: Cornell Institute for Research and Development in Occupational Education, 1975. [ERIC ED 103069].

A total of 1,341 male and female students enrolled at a private women's college, a moderately-sized comprehensive college, an agricultural-technical college, and a small comprehensive college were surveyed to determine demographic and descriptive data, career choices, plans for labor force participation, and perceptions of counseling services. Twice as many women as men were sampled. Analysis of the data revealed that these women were more like the four-year college women than "new students" at two-year colleges. The majority of women studied were 18 or 19 years old, single, and white. Nearly half of both their mothers and fathers had completed some college. While attending college the women depended on their parents for financial support and did not work. Their most common majors were liberal arts, health sciences, or secretarial science. Unlike four-year college women, however, their occupational choices resembled those of their fathers more than their mothers and they anticipated continuous commitment to work. They selected their careers for special interest, opportunity to work with people, and ability to be creative. True role innovativeness was expressed by only one-fifth of the women sampled. Pertinent literature is reviewed, data is presented, and recommendations for improved counseling services are made.

Muhich, D. Testing hypotheses on behavioral preferences of university women and men with multiple linear regression. *Psychological Reports,* 1975, *37*(3), 707–716.

Provides useful statistics on how men and women students vary on achievement orientation, dependency needs, emotional expression, and educability across four broad disciplinary clusters, plus a 5th category of "undecided."

Steininger, M. & Eisenberg, E. On different relationships between dogmatism and Machiavellianism among male and female college students. *Psychological Reports,* 1976, *38*(3), 779–782.

Women's scores on the instrument used in this study suggest that women are typically less Machiavellian than men.

Suter, B. & Domino, G. Masculinity-feminity in creative college women. *Journal of Personality Assessment,* 1975, *39*(4), 414–20.

The possible relationship between masculinity and creativity in college women was investigated through a battery of masculinity-femininity scales that tapped both manifest and latent anxiety, factorially derived clusters, and an ipsative measure. Highly creative subjects scored higher on activity and described themselves as more masculine.

Wilson, K.M. Today's women students: New outlooks and new challenges. *Journal of College Student Personnel,* 1975, *16*(5), 376–381.

"Multipurpose surveys of women students, conducted periodically over the past decade in several selective liberal art colleges, provide evidence that today's women students are projecting smaller families, seeking less traditional avenues for career development, and endorsing more liberal views of women's roles than their predecessors. Trends in these important areas and their implications for college authorities are considered in this brief report."

Counseling Women Students: Tools and Techniques

Blaska, B. Women in academe — the need for support groups. *The Journal of the National Association for Women Deans, Administrators, and Counselors,* 1976, *39*(4), 173–177.

After a brief discussion of the myriad of problems faced by women graduate and undergraduate students in their academic and career aspirations the author proposes that women faculty members, students and counselors form support groups to meet the specific needs of women aspiring to professional careers.

Casey, J.J. The development of a leadership orientation on the SVIB for women. *Measurement and Evaluation in Guidance,* 1975, *8*(2), 96–99.

The SVIB was administered to the entire freshmen class at a midwestern college for women. Results showed leaders responded "like" to about 90 percent of the scale items, whereas nonleaders responded "like" to only about 10 percent. The scale is designed to assist counselors in aiding women to plan their extracurricular involvements.

Goldman, R. Sex-differences in the relationships of attitudes toward technology to choice of field of study. *Journal of Counseling Psychology,* 1973, *20*, 412–418.

Goldman found that male and female college students differed significantly in five aspects of attitudes toward technology. Males showed greater mechanical curiosity than did females. The author concluded that attitude inventories might be useful for counseling students. A common norm for counseling both females and males might actually, be detrimental to both.

McEwen, M.K. Counseling women: A review of the research. *Journal of College Student Personnel*, September 1975, *16*(5), 382–388.

> "This review examines the research support for the major recommendations and issues concerning the counseling of women. Conclusions and implications for counselors are drawn from the research. Resources are identified and suggestions offered to counselors for developing skills for counseling in an unbiased fashion and for designing programs to enhance women's development."

Munley, P.H., Fretz, B.R., & Mills, D.H. Female college student's scores on the men's and women's Strong Vocational Interest Blanks. *Journal of Counseling Psychology*, 1973, *20*(3), 285–289.

> This research concludes with the recommendation that both the men's and women's form of the SVIB be used in counseling female college students. By finding out what the individual has in common with other individuals in a range of occupations — be they men or women — a better range of the student's occupational interest can be identified.

Oliver, L.W. Counseling implications of recent research on women. *Personnel and Guidance Journal*, 1975, *53*(6), 430–437.

> Reviews the recent research on women and generalizes from it in ways that may be useful to college counselors. Specifically covered are counselor bias, demographic changes, sex differences, and sex-role stereotypes.

Reid, E.A. Coresidential living: Expanded outcomes for women. *NASPA*, 1976, *13*(4), 44–56.

> A study of matched groups of college women shows that women in coresidential settings have higher self-esteem, less stereotyped conceptions of sex roles, and better relationships with men and women.

VanderWilt, R.B. & Klocke, R.A. Self-actualization of females in an experimental orientation program. *The Journal of the National Association for Women Deans, Administrators, and Counselors*, 1971, *34*(3), 125–129.

> The authors found that in their small sample (N=20), the experimental orientation program contributed significantly to the self-actualization process of female participants. All statistically significant results occurred among females.

College Women and Sports

A report to the legislature on women in athletic programs at the University of California. Berkeley, CA: University of California, 1974. [ERIC ED 100196]

This document presents a summary report on the status of University of California athletic programs and on progress made in expanding opportunities for women. Each of five areas of campus athletic programs is reviewed in some detail for each sex, including: intercollegiate athletics, intramural sports, recreational club sports, physical education activities courses, and general recreation. Information is provided on every participating campus, and general conclusions on systemwide progress are presented.

Association of American Colleges. *What constitutes equality for women in sport? Federal law puts women in the running.* Washington, D.C. : Association of American Colleges, Project on the Status and Education of Women, 1974. [ERIC ED 089640].

This paper outlines some of the issues related to equal opportunity for women in sports, gives examples of some situations that might have to be reassessed, and discusses some of the alternatives that are being proposed. Emphasis is placed on: the educational value of sport; attitudes toward women in sport; the legal mandate for equality for women in noncompetitive programs; what constitutes mixed teams in competitive athletics; single sex teams vs. mixed teams in competitive athletics, the funding of competitive athletic programs; separate-but-equal administrative structures in athletic and physical education departments, and governing associations; and what constitutes equality for women employees in sports.

Lundegren, H. *Motives of college women for participating in physical activities.* University Park, PA: Pennsylvania State University, College of Health and Physical Education, 1974. [ERIC ED 098165]

One hundred and fifty-one college women, 88 non-physical education majors, and 63 physical education majors were given a 75-item q-sort of statements on motives for participation in physical activity and a background questionnaire that elicited demographic data and information on sports activity experience. Five significant activity types were established for the nonmajors, including (a) the appearance conscious, (b) the skill developers, (c) the fitness fadists, (d) the healthy long-livers, and (e) the groupies. Four significant activity types were established for the phsyical education including (a) the straight arrows, (b) the show-offs; (c) the groupies, and (d) the givers. On the basis of this study the author draws the following conclusions: (a) physical education majors are distinguishable from the nonmajors in terms of their experience in intramural and varsity sports on both the high school and college level and by their participation in sports in leisure time and (b) college and junior high school girls are alike.

Sex discrimination and intercollegiate athletics. *Iowa Law Review*, 1975, *61*(2), 420–96.

The nature and pervasiveness of sex-based inequalities within collegiate athletics are reviewed with regard to constitutional mandates as interpreted by Title IX and the proposed Equal Rights Amendment. Special attention is given to the once discredited "separate but equal" doctrine.

Women in Specific Majors

Bisconti, A.S. & Astin, H.S. *Undergraduate and graduate study in scientific fields.* American Council on Education Research Reports, 1973, *8*(3).

Report of a longitudinal study of a national sample of women who entered college in 1961 and 1966. Reports data on academic field chosen, grade point averages earned and length of time to the baccalaureate, persistence into graduate work, sources of financial support, and duration of training to the doctorate.

Davis, S.O. A researcher's-eye view: Women students, technical majors, and retention. *IEEE Transactions on Education*, 1975, *E-18*(1), 25–29.

Report of an exploratory research project at the University of Minnesota's Institute of Technology. Characteristics, persistence statistics, and other useful survey data about women in technical majors.

Frohreich, D.S. How colleges try to attract more women students. *IEEE Transactions on Education*, 1975, *E18*(1), 41–46.

A survey of 130 of the largest engineering schools in the United States (usable n=70) was conducted to learn how women students were attracted to engineering majors; this article reports the results of the survey. Problems in recruitment are discussed and new approaches are suggested.

Gardner, R.E. Women in engineering: The impact of attitudinal differences on educational institutions. *Engineering Education*, 1970, *67*(3), 233–240.

A two-year longitudinal study of men and women entering the college of engineering at Cornell University shows that there was no indication that statistically significant differences in attitudes were followed by behaviors which had a notable impact on the institution, as measured by academic performance, attrition, or field selection.

Hedges, L.V. & Majer, K. Female and minority representation in college majors as a function of mathematics requirements. San Diego, CA: University of California, 1970. [ERIC ED 123979].

> Black female, Chicano female, Asian female and total female enrollment representations as well as total Black, total Chicano and total Asian enrollment representations were determined for undergraduate major areas at seven University of California campuses. The number of mathematics courses required for each major was also determined from the catalog for each campus. Significant negative correlations were found between the number of math courses required for majors and the representation of each female group and total group in the major except Asians. A significant positive correlation was found for all Asian while no significant correlation was found for Asian females. Implications for increasing the representation of women and minorities in professional and academic careers are discussed.

Lee, O.L. & Hall, J.E. Female library science students & occupational stereotype — fact or fiction? *College and Research Libraries,* 1973, *34*(5), 265–267.

> This study compared the mass media stereotype of library science students and librarians against a general college student norm to see whether the pejorative image was "fact or fiction." Both groups were shown to be similar, with prospective librarians ranking more favorably in some cases.

Miner, J.B. Motivation to manage among women: Studies of college women. *Journal of Vocational Behavior,* 1974, *5*(2), 241–250.

> Females in business administration and liberal arts were shown in this study to have lower managerial motivation scores than the comparable male samples; in educational fields no difference was found. These results are discussed in terms of sex discrimination, managerial talent supply, and the vocational guidance of college women. The author concludes that managerial potential in women does exist, but that it is not developed to the same extent as in men at the present time.

Ott, M.D. The men and women of the class of '79. *Engineering Education,* 1976, *67*(3), 226–232.

> Discusses a survey intended to clarify the characteristics of the women students who are now entering engineering schools. The population consisted of all engineering freshmen who entered one of 42 selected schools during the 1975 fall term.

Rezler, A.G. & Buckley, J.M. A comparison of personality types among female student health professionals. *Journal of Medical Education*, 1977, *52*(6), 475–477.

> This study focuses on the personality traits of six groups of women students in medicine, pharmacy, medical technology, physical therapy, dietetics and occupational therapy. Medical students were shown to prefer thought over feeling in their approach to work and people; pharmacy students liked well-planned, routine work; occupational therapy students liked changing situations and flexibility.

Sproule, B. & Mathis, H.F. Recruiting and keeping women engineering students: An agenda for action. *Engineering Education*, 1976, *66*(7), 745–748.

> This paper presents a survey of the techniques used by 29 engineering colleges that have been successful in recruiting and retaining women engineering students. Eight techniques are described for increasing the enrollment of women, including publicizing techniques, counseling efforts, hiring women faculty, and recruiting at the high school level.

Rates of Return

Benham, L. Benefits of women's education within marriage. *Journal of Political Economy*, 1974,*82*(2, partI), s57.

> A data based study which explores a hypothesis about the return to the family unit of investment in women's education. No clear cause-effect relationship is established, but associations between labor market productivity and education of the family unit (husband and wife), beyond those explained by selective mating are established.

Heins, M., Smock, S. Martindale, L. Jacobs, J. & Stein, M. Comparison of the productivity of men and women physicians. *Journal of the American Medical Association*, 1977, (6sl6), 237(23), 2514–2517.

> This study refutes previous findings about the productivity of women physicians and therefore about the value of training more women to meet the nation's health care needs. Female MD's were found to be equally productive as male MD's, with only about ten percent of their total career time since graduation having been taken out for traditionally female role activities. [*See also: Heins, et al., Productivity of women physicians. Journal of the American Medical Association*, 1976, *236*(17), 1961–1964.]

Hoffer, S.N. Private rates of return to higher education for women. *Review of Economics and Statistics*, 1973, *55*(4), 482–486.

> This study is concerned with the impact of higher education on women's earnings. A college degree is shown to be a profitable investment under most alternative patterns of lifetime labor force behavior that were considered. When labor force behavior differences between men and women are held constant, the rate of return to women is greater than the rate of return to white men, for those having completed four years of college.

Woodhall, M. The economic returns to investment in women's education. *Higher Education*, 1973, *2*(3), 275–300.

> Evidence from nine countries indicates, with exceptions, that returns to secondary and higher education are an average of two percentage points lower for women than for men. Nonmonetary benefits are discussed, along with measurement techniques. A large part of the observed benefit differential is due to women's concentration in lower income occupations. The author concludes that the benefit differential is less than suggested, and that it would be further diminished if women were used more equitably in the labor force.

Entire Journal Issues

The Counseling Psychologist, 1973, *4*(1), ENTIRE ISSUE.

> This entire issue is devoted to counseling women. E.M. Westervelt's contribution, "A tide in the affairs of women: the psychological impact of feminism in educated women" raises some especially important questins about the long range effects of feminism among educated women. To date feminist ideology has changed "the sources of guilt and shame and [modified] both the content of conflicts over plans and decisions and the relative strength of various sources of motivation." These are deeply-rooted changes with unpredictable results.

The Counseling Psychologist, 1976, *6*(2), ENTIRE ISSUE.

> This entire issue is devoted to "Counseling Women," and contains several theory-based and empirically-based papers on the topic, including:
> — Unger, R.K. Male is greater than female: The socialization of status inequality.
> — Harris, D.V. Physical sex differences: A matter of degree.
> — Farmer, H.S. What inhibits achievement and career motivation in women.

— Knefilkamp, L.L., *et al.* Cognitive-developmental theory: A guide to counseling women.
— Jeffries, D.C. Counseling for the strengths of black women.
— Tanney, N.F. & Birk, J.M. Women counselors for women clients? A review of the research.

The Journal of the National Association for Women Deans, Administrators, and Counselors, 1974(Fall), *38*(1), ENTIRE ISSUE.

This issue s devoted to counseling women, and includes research articles on:
— Parrish, J.P. Women, careers and counseling.
— Herman, M.H. & Sedlacek, W.E. Female university student and staff perceptions of rape.
— Hudson, J.M., Henze, L.F., & Hall, M.A. Changing sex standards for the college female.
— Penn, J.R. Female student attitudes — no gap here.

The Journal of the National Association for Women Deans, Administrators, and Counselors, 1976(Fall), *40*(1). ENTIRE ISSUE.

This issue is devoted to questions of "being a women in 1976," and subtitled "Selected issues and research." Articles cover:
— Gould, K.H. Discrimination and reverse discrimination.
— Ten Elshof & Mehl. Academic achievement in college women.
— Marple, B.L.N. Adult women students compared with younger students on selected personality variables.
— Piffner, V.T. Composite profile of a top-level California community college women administrator.

The Journal of the National Association for Women Deans, Administrators, and Counselors, 1977(Summer), *40*(4), ENTIRE ISSUE.

This issue is devoted to values, employment, and status of professional women. Pertinent articles cover:
— Scott, P.B. Preparing Black women for nontraditional professions:Some considerations for career counseling.
— Duff, F.C. & Parrish, J.B. Sex differences in employment of college graduates. [A good "suitability of employment" statistical comparison based on unemployment and underemployment rates, job dissatisfaction, job nrelated to major, and median salary is included. Men were consistently favored.]

School Review, 1974,*80*(2). ENTIRE ISSUE.

This issue in its entirety covers women and education. Most contributions are essays; some are research-based. Pertinent contributions include:
— Baumrind, D. From each according to her abiloity (role redefinition).
— Munuchin, P. The schooling of tomorrow's women. (role redefinition).
— Neugarten, B. Education and the life cycle (role redefinition).
— Lynn, D. Determinants of intellectual growth in women. (sources of sex differentiation).
— Husbands, S. Women's place in higher education (factors influencing education and career aspirations of women in higher educations).
— Lefevre, C. The mature woman as graduate student (empirical study of women graduate students' self-concepts).

CHAPTER FOUR

Academic Women: Graduate Students

Introduction

Recent research on women as doctoral students or holders of the doctorate is very limited, and what does exist appears to be rather broadly dissipated. We have attempted to group our entries into the following: 1) a small cluster of studies covering the psycho-social conditions, attitudes, and constraints under which women seek and hold the doctorate; 2) a small cluster of inquiries into the career placements and attributes of women doctorates; 3) several entries on women doctorates or doctoral students vis-a-vis their institution and its structures; and 4) a small section on women in training in specific academic or professional fields.

Differential sex-role training, differential socialization, and the consequent differential expectations of men and women are themes that run through many of the entries in the first cluster. These factors appaer to be at least partially responsible for differences between men and women on variables such as productivity, assimilation into graduate work, persistence, success, etc. The second cluster provides statistical profiles of women's doctoral and post-doctoral careers, and also examines important elements in shaping women's professional careers, such as quality of first career placements. Entries in the remaining two clusters share a common concern with discrimination against women and the means of reducing it.

Acker, S. Sex differences in graduate student ambition: Do men publish while women perish? *Sex Roles,* 1977, *3*(3), 285–299.

> The conditions under which women graduate students at one British university equal or surpass men in ambition to publish and engage in related behaviors were shown in this study to be aspiration for the doctorate, survival past the second year of study, and possession of non-traditional attitudes towards women's roles.

Baird, L.L. *Entrance of women to graduate and professional education.* Paper presented at the Annual Meeting of the American Psychological Association, Chicago, Illinois, August, 1975.

> The rates at which men and women attend graduate and professional school were compared using a large national sample of college seniors followed up a year after graduation. Women attended less often, even those with very high grades, and were represented most sparsely in law and medicine. A long-term lower level of confidence among women is suggested as a reason.

Bell, J.B. & Bodden, B.F. Myth of the feminist revolution: Future orientation, career revokability, and role reciprocity among female graduate students. *Sociological Focus,* 1972, *5*(2), 55–70.

> The revolution in role definitions suggested in career research has not taken place according to this study of 15 women graduate assistants and their husbands. An inability to reciprocate roles suggests little possibility of creative change in role obligations, and raises questions about the value to society of graduate education for most women. The great waste of intelligent women as a national resource is likely to continue.

Daniels, A.K. *A survey of research concerns on women's issues.* Washington, D.C.: American Association of Colleges, 1975.

> A review of the current state of interest in research on women's issues, based on a six-month National Science Foundation study. While the review is neither comprehensive nor representative of all the ideas and concerns in the area of research on women's issues, it does indicate what kind of work has been done in what areas and provides suggestions on new directions to be explored. Of particular interest to this bibliography is the section on educational socialization in undergraduate, graduate, and professional training (pp. 11–14).

Feldman, S.D. *Escape from the doll's house: Women in graduate and professional school education.* NY: McGraw-Hill, 1974.

>The author concludes, after analyzing massive quantities of data from the Carnegie Commission's National Survey of Faculty and Student Opinion, that prejudiced treatment of women in graduate and professional school is based not uniquely in higher education but largely in the differential socialization patterns prevalent throughout childhood and adolescence.

Feldman, S.D. Graduate study and marital status. *American Journal of Sociology,* 1973, *78*(4), 982–994.

>Conflicts exist between the role of wife and the role of full-time graduate student. Conversely, married male graduate students are the best adjusted of all graduate students. Married men and divorced women are best able to adhere to a career-primacy model.

Garman, L.G. & Plant, W.T. Personality, academic performance, and educational aspirations of very bright women and men vs. those of high average intelligence. *Journal of Genetic Psychology,* 1975, *126*(2), 163–167.

>The IQ independent variable in this study accounted for almost all measured differences between groups; sex difference appeared only on the responsibility scale where women scored significantly higher than men. The authors concluded that more studies are needed using ability level as an independent variable before reported differences are assumed to result from differential sex role training.

Holmstrom, E.I. & Holmstrom, R.W. The plight of the woman doctoral student. *American Educational Research Journal,* 1974, *11*(1), 1–17.

>Women are more likely to withdraw from graduate school than are their male counterparts. Lack of recognition from their professors and lack of interaction with them are the principal reasons. Female role models in senior faculty positions are recommended.

Kjerulff, K.H. & Blood, M. R. Comparison of communication patterns in male and female graduate students. *Journal of Higher Education,* 1973, *44*(8), 623–632.

>Examines communication patterns between female graduate students and their research advisers vs. such patterns in male graduate students. The authors conclude that women graduate students are at a disadvantage in terms of communication with their professors, especially in informal contacts outside the office.

Lefevre, C. The mature woman as graduate student. *School Review,* 1972, *80*(2), 281–297.

> This study was done at the University of Chicago using a sample of 35 women, all married mothers, who chose to return to school for graduate study. The major research questions asked what motivated these women and what correlated with their choices to return to academe. The author found returning women students to be more self-confident, more individualistic, and better supported in their ambitions by their husbands than their nonacademic counterparts.

Newman, J.E. Sex differences in organizational assimilation of beginning graduate students in psychology. *Journal of Educational Psychology,* 1974, *66*(1), 129–138.

> The results of this longitudinal study "indicated that female graduate students were significantly less satisfied and assimilated and that they experienced significantly greater role ambiguity and role demands than the males." However role performance (GPA) was comparable. The author suggests the operation of a process — still vague — that affects the role making and role adjustment of beginning psychology graduate students inequitably.

Seater, B.B. & Ridgeway, C.L. Role models, significant others, and the importance of male influence on college women. *Sociological Symposium,* 1976, (Spring), 49–64.

> The effective female role model must not only represent achievement but must also be approved of by men in order to demonstrate a successful resolution of our culture's achievement - femininity conflict. Direct personal encouragement is important to the establishment and maintenance of high educational aspirations, both from men and women. At present, women receive more support from female significant others, but the effect is weaker than encouragement from men. This will change as strong female role models emerge. [N.B.: The entire edition is on the sociology of women.]

Placement and Career

Astin, H. Career profiles of women doctorates. In Rossi & Calderwood (Eds.), *Academic women on the move.* New York: Russel Sage Foundation, 1973.

> This chapter is based on Astin's previous work, *The Woman Doctorate in America* (1969), and on a series of reports on career patterns sponsored by the National Academcy of Sciences. Good comparative statistics across academic fields and time (1960–1970).

Astin, H. *The woman doctorate in America*. New York: Russel Sage Foundation, 1969.

>Extensive statistical survey of 1,547 women who received doctor's degrees in 1957 and 1958. Areas treated include: personal and family characteristics of women doctorates; career choices; career development and work patterns; occupational achievements and awards; home, community, and leisure; obstacles in career development. Also includes some autobiographical sketches and a section on policy implciations.

Cartter, A.M. & Ruhter, W.E. *The disappearance of discrimination in first job placement of new Ph.D's*. Los Angeles: Higher Education Research Institute, 1975. [ERIC ED 104255].

>A well-developed empirical study addressing the prestige and desirability of first post-doctoral placements among men and women. The study concludes that in terms of the quality of the institution at which new doctorates were placed — an important factor in the long-term career development of the new Ph.D. — no evidence of discrimination against women was found for the years 1967–1973.

Centra, J.A. Women with doctorates. *Change,* 1975, 7(1), 48 & 61.

>Capsule summary of a comparative survey of 3,658 men and women doctorates (full report in *Women, Men, and the Doctorate*). Women doctorates have been less likely to reap the rewards enjoyed by their male colleagues.

Centra, J.A. & Kuykendall, N.M. *Women, men, and the doctorate*. Princeton, N.J.: Educational Testing Service, 1974. [ERIC ED 104179].

>This study describes the current status and professional development of a sample of women doctorates and compares them to a sample of men who have attained the same educational status. Chapters cover the sample and procedures used; employment patterns; doctorates in academe; publications, income, and job satisfaction; marriage and family life; graduate school experiences and reactions; attitudes towards women's rights; and summary discussion and implications. Statistical data are presented.

Moore, W.J. & Newman, R.J. An analysis of the quality differentials in male-female academic placements. *Economic Inquiry,* 1977, *15*(3), 413–434.

>This study of quality differences in the academic placements of male and female economists from 1960 to 1974 shows that a 22.2 percent advantage in placement quality accrued to males over females; most of this is attributable to discrimination of some kind. Good further references on status differentials between male and female economists are included.

Attwood, C.L. *Women in fellowship and training programs.* Washington, D.C.: Association of American Colleges, November 1972. [ERIC ED 081371].

> Beginning in June 1972, 68 different fellowship programs sponsored by 28 government agencies, private organizations, and foundations were asked to provide data on the following numbers and percentages of women applicants and women recipients, recruiting and selection procedures, content of application forms, the number of women on selection boards, and policies against sex discrimination. Programs were selected for study mainly on the basis of size and national visibility. Results include: (1) in 1972–1973 about 80% of the nation's most prestigious fellowships and awards went to men. In some of the most competitive programs (Guggenheim fellowships and White House fellows) over 90% are held by men. (2) In a few fellowship programs women have comprised 30% or more of the recipients. (3) Far fewer women than men apply or are nominated for fellowships. (4) The success of women who do apply or are nominated varies widely. (5) Women play an insignificant part in the selection, with many panels having no female members.

Clifford, M.M. & Walster, E. The effect of sex on college admission work evaluation, and job interviews. *Journal of Experimental Education,* 1972, *41*(2), 1–5.

> This research concludes that women are treated inequitably, unless possessed of unusual ability or an existing success record, in all three areas examined: college admissions, ratings of creative productions, employment at the immediate post-doctoral level.

Hochman, L.M. & Nietfeld, C.R. Differences in sources of financing of female and male Michigan State University graduate students. *Journal of College Student Personnel,* 1976, *17*(1), 55–60.

> The authors conclude that while differences currently exist, "when women seek Ph.D's as often as men, begin graduate study directly after receipt of bachelor's degrees, and plan for professional and continuous careers early, they should find as many sources of income open to them as to their male counterparts."

McCarthy, J.H. & Wolfe, D. Doctorates granted to women and minority group members. *Science,* 1975, *189*, 857.

> Association of American Universities member universities are significantly increasing the number of doctoral degrees awarded to women and minority

group members, and are decreasing the number awarded to majority males according to this survey. (Good statistics by field of study.)

Nies, J. *Women and fellowships*. Washington, D.C.: Women's Equity Action League, April 1974. [ERIC ED 091970].

Last year over 80% of the major fellowship awards went to men. There are many reasons that women are not found in higher numbers among fellowship applicants. One of the strongest is that the image of the fellowship recipient is male. Another difficulty is that information about many programs is informal, passing through word-of-mouth networks.

Ninety-nine leading institutions in proportion of Ph.D.'s granted to women, 1973–1976. *The Chronicle of Higher Education*, 1978, *16*(1), 5.

A "fact file" table showing the 99 American institutions which lead in the proportion of Ph.D.'s they award to women.

Sells, L.W. *Preliminary report on the status of graduate women: University of California, Berkeley*. Berkeley, CA: University of California, 1973.]ERIC ED 082636].

The report is divided into six sections: presentation of nationwide, university-wide, and Berkeley data concerning women in graduate school; Berkeley enrollment and degree figures for women; national doctoral production data for women; dropout data for women; affirmative action materials; and data on two pilot studies of high school mathematics preparation concerning the correlation of mathematics success for women with later academic success; and the implications of undergraduate major choice for women.

Solmon, L.C. Women in doctoral education: Clues and puzzles regarding institutional discrimination. *Research in Higher Education*, 1973, *1*(4), 299–332.

The main question of this study is "what evidence would be needed to determine whether or not women graduate students are treated unfairly?" It brings together an extensive collection of tables, charts and graphs on women doctoral students, concluding with a plea for collection of more systematic data by sex.

Training in Specific Fields

Andberg, W.L. Women in veterinary medicine: The myths and the reality. *Journal of Veterinary Medical Education*, 1976, *3*(2), 54–6.

For the years 1969–75, there was no significant difference in the proportions of male and female applicants admitted to the college of veterinary medicine at the University of Minnesota. It is hoped that the sex-typing of veterinary medicine by counselors, teachers, parents, and veterinarians will diminish.

Cartwright, L.K. Conscious factors entering into decisions of women to study medicine. *Journal of Social Issues,* 1972, *28*, 201–215.

This is a study of the motivation and personality of female medical school students. Encouragement from others, long standing interest, self-development motives, and altruism prompt females to enter medical school. In contrast, economic and prestige factors are seldom mentioned.

Cartwright, L.K. Personality differences in male and female medical students. *Psychiatry in Medicine,* 1972, *3*(3), 213–218.

This study shows that women medical students tend to display more sensitivity to relationship values, more general acceptance of feelings, and greater alertness to moral and ethical issues than male medical students. They also value independence and individuality to a greater degree than their male colleagues or educated women in general.

Chronicle of Higher Education, 1978, *15*(18), 15.

Page 15 of this issue contains a comparison chart showing women's progress in four professional fields: medicine, dentistry, veterinary medicine, and law. Steady progress in all fields is shown for the period 1969–1976, although the totals are not all impressive.

Dube, W.F. Women's enrollment and its minority component in U.S. medical schools. *Journal of Medical Education,* 1976, *51*(8), 691–693.

Statistics on women in American medical schools. The percentage of women medical school applicants from 1930–1970 rose from four to eleven percent; the rise in women applicants from 1970–1975 was twice the previous figures. While male enrollments increased 5% from 1971–1972 to 1975–1976, the enrollment of women enrollments rose 140%. Further increases in women's enrollments can be expected, but at a slower pace.

Increase in women law students. *Intellect,* 1974, *102*, 489–90.

This entry provides good comparative statistics (to 1973) on women law students, and documents the dramatic rise in female applicants and matriculants at U.S. law schools.

Oltman, R.M. *Status of graduate and professional education of women — 1974: A review of the literature and bibliography.* Paper presented for the American Association of University Women Conference on Graduate and Professional Education of Women, May 9–10, 1974. [ERIC ED 092022].

This document reviews the status of graduate and professional education of women for 1974. The first section, a review of the literature, discusses background and current developments, the status of graduate education, reports concerning women in higher education, social factors and attitudes, institutional barriers, trends in specific disciplines, requirements of the law, and proposed solutions. The second section encompasses a 68-item bibliography on graduate and professional education of women.

Parrish, J.B. Women in professional training. *Monthly Labor Review*, 1974, 97, 41–43.

Presents statistics on the topic.

Rosen, R.A.H. Occupational role innovators and sex role attitudes. *Journal of Medical Education*, 1974, 49(6), 554–561.

It was found that women in medical schools support the option of careers for women generally, although not necessarily at the expense of the maternal role. This pattern was stronger among students than faculty members.

Strober, M.H. Women economists: Career aspirations, education, and training. *American Economic Review*, 1975, 65(2), 92–99.

The characteristics of women economists are presented in a statistical portrait which includes such variables as undergraduate and graduate education.

Why women need their own MBA programs. *Business Week*, 1974, (February 23), 102–103.

Popular report of a new program at Simmons College (Boston) to train women for corporate management, and a good expose of why such programs may be necessary or helpful.

CHAPTER FIVE

Academic Women: Administrators

Introduction

Research on women in academic administration is remarkably sparse, undoubtedly owing both to the relative scarcity of such women and the short span of time since research awareness has turned to this sector of academe. Particularly in the case of women trustees, there has been a nearly total lack of research effort.

As in the other major divisions of the bibliography, a substantial portion of the research here concerns itself with questions of male/female equality. The issues of sex discrimination among administrators, unequal compensation, and discrimination in hiring and the delegation of responsibilities are the best treated issues, and they reach the predictable conclusion that equality has yet to be achieved.

Questions about women's role and characteristics of women administrators arise in three entries and also in one of the articles comprising a special issue of the *The Journal of the National Association for Women Deans, Administrators, and Counselors* on academic women.

Items on leadership development — how to do it and examples of programs underway — comprise perhaps the most interesting cluster. An extensive bibliography on women in management is included because the constructs that have been applied in studying women as leaders in business may well transfer to the context of higher education where a conceptual base for such research is conspicuously lacking.

Top level women administrators in the community college is the subject of two entries, the effects of women and minority members on boards of trustees is treated in one entry, and a review of the literature is also included. The literature review, interestingly, deals principally with material in doctoral dissertations; this indicates that perhaps in coming years more research in the topic will appear as the authors of the dissertations in question continue their research in a professional capacity.

Discrimination

Kaufmann, S.G. Few women get positions of power in academe, survey discloses. *The Chronicle of Higher Education,* 1970, *5*(10), 1 & 4.

> A statistical report on the distribution of women in policy making positions in academe. Women attain higher status in private and/or small colleges.

Magarrell, J. Who earns how much in academe? *The Chronicle of Higher Education,* 1975, *9*(19), 1.

> Good presentation and discussion of NCES Statistics on average full-time faculty salaries in 1974–75 by (1) public/private institutions, (2) men/women, (3) faculty rank and type of institution (2 year, 4 year, university). Also gives two-year increase in salary from 1972–1973 to 1974–1975, and women's share of faculty jobs across all ranks for the same period.

Intellect, 1973, *102*(2352), 132–133.

> This study compares men and women administrators in schools of education on variables of proportional representation, professional preparation, background experiences, current responsibilities and social interaction orientation. Methodology is treated very lightly, but authors find that except for the orientation-to-social-interaction variable, women and men differ considerably.

Mattfeld, J. *Many are called, but few are chosen.* Paper presented at the 55th Annual Meeting of the American Council on Education, 1972. [ERIC ED 071549]

> There are three general categories of administrators in the Ivy League and most other schools: (1) those who are employed to maintain and develop the phsyical plant, to manage the business operations, alumnae and other public relations, and development; (2) those who work in admissions, financial aid, student affairs, the academic and personal counseling of students, placement, and the registrar's office; and (3) the academic leaders of the university such as the president, chancellors, provosts, and the deans of faculties, colleges, graduate and professional schools, and special programs. Women have traditionally been held from the ranks of those who are hired for administrative positions in universities. However, the solution to this unequal practice is seen to be easily solved in all except the last of the administrative categories. This document reviews the past and present history related to women in administrative positions in the Ivy League schools, and offers hopes for further equality of opportunity in such positions.

Reeves, M.E. An analysis of job satisfaction of women administrators in higher education. *The Journal of the National Association for Women Deans, Administrators, and Counselors*, 1975, *38*(3), 132–135.

    The working climate has not changed appreciably for most women in administrative positions. Job satisfaction seems to come from a sense of personal worth rather than from a working climate.

Schetlin, E.M. Wonderland and looking-glass: Women in administration. *The Journal of the National Association for Women Deans, Administrators, and Counselors*, 1975, *38*(3), 104–109.

    The author delineates several problems in dealing with sex discrimination among college administrators.

The status of women faculty and administrators in higher educational institutions, 1971–1972. National Education Association Research Memo No. 1973–7. Washington D.C.: National Education Association, 1973.

    This research memo provides a brief report of the status of women faculty and administrators in higher education based on three types of information collected in the NEA Research biennial study of salaries in higher education in 1971–72. In addition to summarizing faculty salaries by sex, this memo reports the tenure status of faculty by sex and reviews the number of persons and their salaries by sex in administrative positions in higher education. Information about the coverage and format of the biennial study, along with detailed tables of faculty salary information by sex, is given in the report of the 1971–72 study.

Van Alstyne, C., Mensel, R.F., Withers, J.S., & Malott, F.S. *1975–76 Administrative Compensation Survey. Women and minorities in administration of higher educational institutions*. Washington D.C.: College and University Personnel Association, 1977.

    This study is the first comprehensive analysis of higher education administration, based on a national survey, to compare the employment patterns and salary levels of women and minorities with those of white men. Over 2700 institutions are included in the survey. Overall, the findings confirmed that employment patterns vary substantially by sex and race, and that salary differentials are more consistently related to sex than to race.

Van Alstyne, C., Withers, J.S. Elliot, S.A. Affirmative inaction: The bottom line tells the tale. *Change*, 1977, *9*(8), 39–41.

    A distillation of the essential material from Van Alstyne *et. al.* (1977) reported above.

Women administrators found unequal in pay status. *The Chronicle of Higher Education,* 1977, *14*(16), 8.

> Key findings of two major surveys of women administrators in the nation's colleges and universities include the following:
> — equivalent titles (in equivalent institutions) held by women and men are remunerated unequally; women earn 20% less than men.
> — only 16% of key administrative positions at institutions surveyed were held by women (14% white women vs. 2% minority women).
> — affirmative action officer is the only job title where sizable representation of women and men, minorities and whites occurred.
> — male affirmative action officers are paid more than women in that position.
> N.B.: One of these surveys is based on the same data appearing in Van Alstyne (1977) in this section of the Bibliography.]

Roles and Characteristics

Arter, M.H. *The role of women in administration in state universities and land-grant colleges.* 1973 [ERIC ED 086085]

> This study investigated the role of women in the administration of state universities and land-grant colleges. Findings and conclusions were based on 146 usable responses from chief officers of multi-campus institutions and 101 responses from women in top-level administrative positions. Various background variables were shown to be related to the position, salary, and academic rank of women in top-level administrative positions. Among the relevant variables are such things as geographical regions of employment and birth, the occupation of their fathers, the education of their mothers, the type of institution attended at the master's and doctoral level, the holding of a doctoral degree, what they thought helped them gain their positions, to whom they were directly responsible, for what they were responsible, whether they carried out policy or transmitted decisions, and the availability of tenure as administrators.

Epstein, C.R. *Woman's place.* Berkeley, CA: University of California Press, 1970.

> Discusses female socialization and reconciliation to the roles of women. Includes studies on the barriers for women's achieving professional status. The thrust of the book is directed toward the examination of the attitudes which have hindered advancement of women.

Horner, M.S. Femininity and successful achievement: A basic inconsistency. In Garskof, M.H. (Ed), *Roles women play: Readings toward women's liberation.* Belmont, CA: Brooks/Cole Publishing Company, 1971.

> "Discussess achievement-motivation research using female subjects in

which social conditions of testing have been found to be an important variable." (p. 61)

The Journal of the National Association for Women Deans, Administrators, and Counselors, 1976 (Summer), *39*(4). Entire issue.

This entire issue is devoted to academic women: past, present and future. Research articles include:

(1) Johnson, J. & O'Brien, C.R. Women presidents: The first 50 years [study of the background of 34 women presidents of the American Personnel and Guidance Association and its divisions.]

(2) Blaska, B. Women in academe — the need for support groups. [see separate entry]

(3) McBee, M.L., Murray, R. & Suddick, D.E. Self esteem differences of professional women [found that women in traditionally masculine-oriented endeavors have higher self-esteem than those in feminine roles.]

Leadership Development

Gordon, R.S. & Ball, P.G. Survival dynamics for women in educational administration. *The Journal of the National Association for Women Deans, Administrators, and Counselors*, 1977, *40*(2), 46–48.

Not research *per se*, but a good assessment of what is needed for women to succeed in higher education administrative positions including the nature of support groups.

Haines, J. & Penny, S. (Eds.) *Women and management in higher education.* Report of a conference sponsored by the Office of Higher Education Management Services, New York State Education Department and State University of New York, December 1973.

Papers focus on (1) "current" attitudes and activities relative to women in higher education management positions; (2) methods for enlarging the female candidate pool for administrative positions; (3) the conditions under which women function in higher education management; (4) current affirmative action plans and future prospects. Some are research-based.

Kaye, B. & Scheele, A. Leadership training. *New Directions for Higher Education*, 1975, *3*, 79–93.

A survey of 60 programs to prepare women for leadership in business and education identifies two distinct types of skills training (life-building skills and technical and managerial skills) and offers ideas to institutions planning leadership programs. Six model programs are described and 24 are listed in the bibliography.

Oster, R.G. The Claremont women administrators program: The grooming of an administratrix. *Bulletin of the Association of Departments of Foreign Languages,* 1975, 7(1), 39–42.

While underlining the need for more women in administrative positions in higher education, the paper describes the Claremont women administrators program, a three-year pilot program offering practical experience in academic administration to women qualified for administrative careers. One internship is described in detail and the program is evaluated.

Sandmeyer, L., Kohn, P., Driscoll, J.B. Harrison, C.H., & Sagaria, M.A.D. *A program for optimizing women's leadership skills.* Washington D.C.: National Association for Women Deans, Administrators, and Counselors, 1977.

A useful document comprising sections on (1) the history of women in leadership roles, (2) the literature regarding women and leadership, and (3) current leadership programs (including the OWLS — Optimizing Women's Leadership Skills program). Also included is an extensive annotated bibliography on women and leadership.

Shapiro, E., Haseltine, F.P., & Rowe, M.P., Moving up: Role models, mentors and the patron system. *Sloan Management Review,* 19, 8(Spring, 1975), 51–58.

A provocative analysis and discussion of the way sponsored mobility into top positions in academe may operate. The authors suggest a continuum of relationships from lesser to greater intimacy and importance.

Touchter, J., & Shavlik, D. Challenging the assumptions of leadership: Women and men of the academy. *New Directions in Higher Education* (22), Washington, D.C.: 1978.

A discussion based on extensive observation of top-level academic leaders which disarms a number of myths concerning the ability of women to fill these posts. The authors provide several suggestions for removing barriers to greater utilization of women, including monitoring and sponsorship opportunities.

Williams, M., Oliver, J.S., & Gerrard, M. *Women in management: A bibliography.* Austin TX: Center for Social Work Research. School of Social Work, 1977.

> Selected bibliography on recent literature divided into eight topical areas, each with a brief introduction. The section entitled *women as leaders* is especially rich in providing access to the literature on women in upper administrative positions in business. Constructs from the business area may well transfer to higher education administration, however.

Miscellaneous

Goerss, K.v.W. *Women administrators in education: A review of research 1960–1976.* Washington, D.C.: National Association for Women Deans, Administrators, and Counselors, 1977.

> Review of the literature of women in education administration roles. Most of the entries are doctoral dissertations, indicating (a) that very little research besides doctoral dissertations has been on the topic, and (b) that we might conceivably be seeing more on the topic if the dissertation authors in question continue their line of research.

Hartnett, R.T. *The new college trustee: Some predicitions for the 1970s. A research consideration of some of the possible outcomes of greater diversity on college governing boards.* Princeton, NJ: Educational Testing Service, 1970.

> Significant changes have taken place since 1968 in the composition of many college and university governing boards. Members of groups previously not well represented on boards of trustees — Blacks, women, and people under age 40 — have been added in considerable numbers. This study draws on data gathered in a 1969 national survey of over 5,000 trustees (see *College and university trustees: their backgrounds, roles, and educational attitudes*. Educational Testing Service, 1969), and examines in detail the characteristics of these previously underrepresented subgroups. It is concluded that continued increases of these people on college governing boards will probably tend to have a liberalizing influence on the overall orientations of most boards of trustees.

Moore, K.M. (Ed). *Gateways and barriers for women in the university community.* Proceedings of the Mary Donlon Alger Conference for Trustees and Administrators. Ithaca, N.Y.: Cornell University, 1976.

> One of the first conferences organized by women trustees to consider the status and problems of women in academe. Contains an extensive annotated bibliography, including a list of periodicals that follow affirmative action.

Pfiffner, V.T. Women as leaders in higher education in these changing times. *The Delta Kappa Gamma Bulletin*, 1975, *41*(3), 5–10.

> Summary article from author's Ph.D. dissertation on 22 top-level female administrators in California's community colleges. Conclusions of the research are listed, and recommendations are provided.

Thurston, A.J. A woman president? — A study of two-year college presidents. *The Journal of the National Association for Women Deans, Administrators, and Counselors*, 1975, *38*(3), 118–123.

> A survey of the women presidents of nine junior colleges reveals some interesting insights regarding women as chief administrators.

CHAPTER SIX

Academic Women: Faculty

Introduction

Our entries on *faculty women* are divided into five subcategories or subheadings. These are 1) discrimination, 2) strategies and instruments used in discovering and reducing discrimination, 3) women in specific disciplines, 4) women academics vs. men academics: traits, state, productivity and success, and 5) general status studies.

Under the first subheading, *discrimination,* expository pieces appear covering both the educational and operational facets of academic discrimination against women. Operational facets of discrimination in hiring, salary and benefits, promotion and tenure, quality of institution, and opportunities to participate in governance. Three British entries provide a point of comparison and suggests that U.S. higher education has not been alone in discriminating against women academics.

The second subcategory encompasses entries ranging from suggested methods for determining the level and intensity of discriminatory practices on campus to lawsuits and their apparently limited effectiveness; from collective bargaining as a femininist weapon in academe to the power of female protest. Only one entry focuses on departmental rather than central administration power in matters of academe, and grapples with the means of anti-discrimination at this fundamental and critically important level.

The third section covers a wide range of status reports from individual disciplines or disciplinary clusters, as well as research conducted on only one disciplinary group of academic women. Items applicable to the other subcategories are found in this section if they cover only one discipline or disciplinary cluster. Representation across the disciplinary spectrum is fair, but the quality of entries across the disciplines is somewhat uneven. Despite this, the statistical presentations in most pieces are good, and suggest nearly universal discrimination against women in academic disciplines and applied fields.

Under the fourth subheading are grouped a series of entries, many of which compare women and men (overtly or tacitly) on what we have called traits, states, productivity, and success. The productivity and success elements refer to the usual scholarly measures for these attributes: publishing, promotion and tenure. "Traits" refers broadly to ascribed attitudes and values and to "characterize" experiences of women academics that may relate to differences in success, productivity, sense of satisfaction, etc. "States" refers to attributes or conditions such as age, race or disciplinary training that may also relate to success, productivity, sense of satisfaction, etc.

The fifth section, general status studies on women faculty, is largely self-explanatory. Many of these studies or reports are association-based, one is geographically-based (New York State), one or two are independent, and one or two are government based. Whereas most of these entries peg the status of women at the time the study was undertaken, Kilson (1976) goes an uncomfortable but necessary step further to analyze what the status of women in American higher education is likely to be in the future given a declining college population and restrictive economy. Two items dealing tangentially with faculty women are appended to this section, although they defy classification even in this location. One addresses the issue of faculty wives, and the other assesses attitudes toward professional couples.

Discrimination

Abramson, J. *The invisible woman.* San Francisco: Jossey-Bass, 1975.

>Personal case history of the author's sex discrimination case with the University of Hawaii. Contains a penetrating analysis of academic process and procedures.

Allen, I.L. & Wilkie, J.R. Commuting married faculty women and the traditional academic community. *Sociological Symposium,* 1976, *17*. 33–44.

>This paper "focuses on the characteristics of some academic communities that operate as barriers to commuters, and discusses why these barriers operate selectively against married women."

Astin, H.S. & Bayer, A.E. Sex discrimination in academe. *Educational Record,* 1972, *53*(2), 101–118.

>Statistical study of sex discrimination in the academic reward system using salary, rank, and tenure as indicators. Proposes a reevaluation of the reward system, since it serves to discriminate not only against women, but against students in general as well.

Bayer, A.E. & Astin, H.S. Sex differentials in the academic reward system. *Science,* 1975, *188*(4190), 796–802.

>Presents national estimates of current sex differentials in academic employment and of the extent to which equity has been approached since antibias regulations have been in effect, 1968–1969. Three criterion variables were used: academic rank, tenure status, and base institutional salary.

Bernstein, M.C. & Williams, L.G. Professor Higgins' complaint, or the pension treatment of women who refuse to act like men. *Educational Record,* 1974, *55*(4), 248–256.

>   Discusses the impact of federal anti-discrimination laws on group pension plans. The authors examine several strategies for ending pension discrimination without undermining the precarious financial position of institutions.

Coates, T.J. & Southern, M.J. Differential educational aspiration levels of men and women undergraduate students. *The Journal of Psychology,* 1972, *81*(1), 125–128.

>   In this investigation of elements contributing to the underrepresentation of women in academe (departments of psychology in this case), women were found to have lower educational aspiration than men despite equivalent intellectual capacity. The authors conclude that this lower aspiration, and not discrimination alone, accounts for the dearth of women academics.

Faia, M.A. Discrimination and exchange: Double burden of the female academic. *Pacific Sociological Review,* 1977, *20*(1), 3–20.

>   This article considers some of the subtler dimensions of sex bias with which female academics are faced: discrimination not only in terms of salary, but also prestige of institution, rank, tenure status, the personal costs of attaining and keeping an academic career, etc.

Farber, S. Earnings and promotion of women faculty. *American Economic Review,* 1977, *67*(2), 199.

>   A unique longitudinal study of sex differences in academic rank, promotion, and earings. Provides interesting variations in the patterns of promotion and earnings of women academics at various age levels, but finds that women do receive lower compensation than males, and that they have significantly lower chances of promotion at all ranks and ages. A limitation is that the study uses 1960–1966 data. Includes a good but brief review of literature on the topic.

Ferber, M.A. & Huber, J.A. Sex of student and instructor: A study of student bias. *American Journal of Sociology,* 1975, *80*, 949–963.

>   The results of this study of 1,291 college students challenge Goldberg's widely cited conclusion that women discriminate against women professionals. Here, men students evaluated male professors more favorably than female professors, and women students did the opposite.

Flanders, J. The use and abuse of part-time faculty. *Bulletin of the Association of Departments of Foreign Languages,* (Special joint issue with *Bulletin of the Association of Departments of English,* No. 50 September 1976), 1976, *8*(1), 49–52.

The practice of hiring part-time faculty at many colleges and universities and the discriminatory treatment they often receive in salary, tenure, and other employment conditions are described.

Hollon, C.J. & Gemmill, G.R. A comparison of female and male professors on participation in decision-making, job-related tension, job involvement, and job satisfaction. *Educational Administration Quarterly,* 1976, *12*(1), 80–93.

This comparative study is based on perceptions from 321 community college faculty. Women perceive less participation in decision-making, less job involvement, less job satisfaction, and greater job-related tension than men.

Goldstein, J.M. Affirmative action: Equal employment rights for women in academia. *Teachers College Record,* 1973, *74*(3), 395–422.

Excellent and comprehensive analysis of the evolving relationship between institutions of higher education and the federal government in the area of sex discrimination, and what it implies for higher education in coming years.

Ingram, A. *Beliefs of women faculty about discrimination.* 1973. [Mimeo available from author, Department of Physical Education, Cole Field House, University of Maryland, 20740.]

This entry presents the results of a questionnaire survey of faculty women at the University of Maryland (Spring, 1973) concerning sex discrimination. The major conclusions are (1) that faculty women at the University of Maryland feel their difficulties are individual and do not know that other women are experiencing similar difficulties, and (2) female concern over failure to obtain aspirations is prevalent, but not apparent to the "male chain of command."

Johnson, G.E. & Stafford, F.P. The earnings and promotion of women faculty. *American Economic Review,* 1974, *64*(6), 888–903.

The major conclusions of this study are that while men and women academics start at roughly comparable salaries in the six disciplines studied (women begin at 4% - 11% less), the differential 15 years after completion of the doctorate is substantial (13% - 23% less). Also women are more likely to be employed by teaching-oriented rather than research-oriented institutions. The authors discuss the meaning of the evidence presented, and calculate that only two-fifths of the salary differential over a 35 year career is due to discriminatory practices *per se*. The remaining three-fifths may be explainable by simple market reactions to voluntary choices by females.

Keiffer, M.G. & Cullen, D.M. *Women who discriminate against other women: The process of denial*. Know, Inc., Pittsburgh, PA, no date. (c.1972)

Documents sex discrimination in academic psychology based on a questionnaire survey of Ph.D. psychologists employed in academic settings.

Koch, J.V. & Chizmar, J.F., Jr. Sex discrimination and affirmative action in faculty salaries. *Economic Inquiry*, 1976, *14*(1), 16–24.

The results of this study at Illinois State University show (1) that sex-based salary discrimination existed before affirmative action plans were implemented, (2) that salary discrimination against women no longer exists after affirmative action implementation, (3) that productivity variables and performance are significnat predictors of salary, (4) that after affirmative action implementation there is significant salary discrimination against men, and (5) affirmative action effects are complex and must be closely monitored.

Lester, R.A. *Antibias regulation of universities: Faculty problems and their solutions*. New York: McGraw Hill, 1974.

A comprehensive inquiry into the issue of ending discrimination against women and minorities in higher education employment and advancement. The author supports the end but not the means (i.e. federal affirmative action policies) of ending bias in academic employment. [See also Lester, R.A. The fallacies of numerical goals. *Educational Record*, 1976, *57*(1), 58–64.rb

Liss, L. Why academic women do not revolt: Implication for affirmative action. *Sex Roles*, 1975, *1*(3), 209–223.

"The study highlights the irony of the way women perceive their status and their own documentation of the day to day inequities which cumulatively result in the statistical patterns now accepted by the U.S. Supreme Court as *prima facie* evidence of sex discrimination." Reasons for the imperceptions include concentration in the lowest ranks, pluralistic ignorance, merit myths, and cooptation.

Loeb, J. & Ferber, M. Sex as predictive of salary and status on a university faculty. *Journal of Educational Measurement*, 1971, *8*(4), 235–244.

In this study (usable response of only about 30%), "sex added significantly to the predictability of salary beyond that achieved by multiple measures of merit and experience..." The existence of discrimination against women both in salary and rank is supported.

Mackie, M. Students' perceptions of female professors. *Journal of Vocational Behavior*, 1976, *8*(3), 337–348.

> Female professors in this study were perceived as more competent than males in task and socioemotional competence. Males were not regarded as having significantly higher prestige, even among female students who have been characterized as being prejudiced against their own sex.

Magarrel, J. Who earns how much in academe? *The Chronicle of Higher Education*. 1975, *9*(19), 1.

> Good presentation and discussion of NCES statistics on average full-time faculty salaries in 1974–75 by: 1) public/private control; 2) sex; 3) faculty rank and type of institution (2 year, 4 year, university). Also gives two-year increase in salary from 1972–1973 to 1974–1975, and women's share of faculty jobs across all ranks for the same period.

Masterman, M. Falling through the grid, or what has happened to the scarce women academics. *Journal for the Theory of Social Behavior*, 1974, *4*(1), 97–107.

> A panoramix grid (see Blackwell, *Times Higher Education Supplement*, 3/16/73) was constructed on the decreasing number of women in high academic positions. The outcomes reaffirmed academic discrimination and demonstrated a new method of analysis.

Mayfield, B. & Nash, W.R. Career attitudes of female professors. *Psychological Reports*, 1976, *39*(2), 631–634.

> Women professors at Texas A&M indicated in a survey that they had benefitted from their career in terms of financial gain, personal fulfillment, and increased opportunities. Very little sex discrimination or personal and family conflict were reported.

Peters, D.S. *And pleasantly ignore my sex: Academic women, 1974*. Ann Arbor, MI: Center for the Study of Higher Education, 1974.

> This essay provides a synoptic review of the research literature on academic women, concluding that the research collectively demonstrates both society's and higher education's discrimination against professional academic women. Includes a good bibliography.

Rendel, M. Men and women in higher education. *Educational Review*, 1975, *27*(3), 192–201.

> A position paper on sex discrimination in British higher education. The author argues that there is discrimination, that it is cumulative, that it is widespread throughout academe (admissions policies, acceptance for advanced degrees, access to prestigious positions, pay, promotion and research awards), and that it is unacceptable in a publicly financed "community of scholars."

Roberts, S. *Equality of opportunity in higher education — the impact of control compliance and the Equal Rights Amendment.* Washington, D.C.: National Organization for Women, 1972. [ERIC ED 074920.]

> Women are not hired and promoted at the same rate, nor have they been paid as well as their male counterparts in higher education. In October 1972, HEW issued the higher education guidelines that called for (1) nondiscriminatory practices in hiring and promotion of women and minorities in higher education, and (2) affirmative action programs to assure that any discriminatory practices in existence will be eradicated. Colleges and universities can now take one of two courses of action. They can either listen to the demands and charges of women and attempt to rectify whatever adverse conditions exist, or they can ignore such demands and face possible legal proceedings.

Sandler, B. Backlash in academe: A critique of the Lester Report. *Teachers College Record*, 1975, *76*: 401–419.

> A point by point rebuttal to the Lester Report. [Lester, R.A. *Antibias regulation of universities.* Report for the Carnegie Commission on Higher Education. N.Y.: McGraw Hill, 1974.]

Shoemaker, E.A. & McKeen, R.L. Affirmative action and hiring practices in higher education. *Research in Higher Education*, 1975, *3*(4), 359–64.

> Data from 191 institutions which placed notices in the *Chroncile of Higher Education* revealed that there are qualified minority and female candidates available for employment and that members of minority groups are making progress toward employment while white males are not being "closed out" of the hiring process.

Steele, C.M. & Green, S.G. Affirmative action and hiring: A case study of value conflict. *Journal of Higher Education*, 1976, *47*(4), 413–435.

> A case study at the University of Washington of the conflict between university compliance with the values of affirmative action and resistance to the Federal mandate requiring compliance with affirmative action regulations.

Tables of salaries and tenure of full-time instructional faculty, 1974–75. Wasington, D.C.: National Center for Educational Statistics. [ERIC ED 104208]

The data presented in this pamphlet are from the survey of salaries and tenure of full-time instructional faculty for 1974–1975. Tables 1–4 show mean salaries of instructional faculty by rank, sex, and level of institution; Table 5 shows the percentage of women among the full-time instructional faculty by control and level of institution in the 50 states and the District of Columbia; Table 6 shows the percentage of full-time instructional faculty with tenure, by institutional control, sex, and state or the other area. These tables seem to indicate that: (1) the mean salaries of instructional faculty employed for the academic year rose approximately 10.5 percent from 1972 to 1974; (2) Salaries at the publicly controlled institutions rose faster than at the privately controlled; (3) The salaries of women relative to men have not significantly improved in two years; (4) The disadvantages of women were also reflected in the tenure situation, where 26.7 percent of the women and 57.0 percent of the men had tenure.

Tanur, J.M. & Coser, R.L. Pockets of poverty in the salaries of academic women. *American Association of University Professors Bulletin,* 1978, *64*(1), 26–30.

Using standard statistical methods but also a special analysis of patterns of underpayment, the authors attempt to identify possible "pockets of poverty" that are usually washed out by the use of standard statistical methods. Conclusive evidence was not produced, but speculative conclusions about where such "pockets" lie are offered.

Strategies and Instruments Related to Discrimination and its Reduction

Bergman, B.R. & Maxfield, M., Jr. How to analyze the fairness of faculty women's salaries on your campus. *AAUP Bulletin,* 1975 *61*, 262–265.

A prototype study of faculty salaries at the University of Maryland was conducted using a methodology considered applicable on other campuses. Computer analysis of data on salaries and faculty characteristics using a multiple regression equation for predicting male and female salaries produced results showing sex biased salary-setting procedures.

Clark, D.R. Discrimination suits: A unique settlement. *Educational Record,* 1977, *58*(3), 233–249.

The case history of a class action suit by five women faculty against Montana State University in 1976. The suit alleged "discrimination in pay and promotion, as well as underrepresentation and underutilization of women faculty members as a class." The settlement and how it was reached is discussed.

Divine, T.M. Women in the academy: Sex discrimination in university faculty hiring and promotion. *Journal of Law and Education,* 1976, *5*(4), 429–451.

Two models of university hiring practices are proposed and analyzed: the original model and a new model termed the "skill pool" model. The merits and faults of each model are discussed and a case made for the conceptual and legal superiority of the skill pool model for university faculty recruitment. [N.B.: Contains a concise thorough account of antidiscrimination legislation from Title VII of the Civil Rights Act of 1964 to Executive Order 11375(1974).]

Fields, C.M. Courts are rejecting most charges of sex bias made by women professors. *The Chronicle of Higher Education,* 1977, *15*(4), 1, 14.

Fields reports that recent court decisions rejecting females' charges of discrimination have raised doubts about the utility of pressing such claims in court. Three cases are reviewed and conclusions drawn.

Fields, C.M. Federal probes into sex discrimination provoke controversy on campus. *Chronicle of Higher Education,* 1971, *5*(24), 1–2.

Lengthy article on the work being done by such groups as WEAL and NOW in conjunction with HEW to end discrimination against academic women.

Gray, M.W. Report of Committee W, 1975–76. *AAUP Bulletin,* 1976, *62*(2), 192–4.

Progress made by academic women in eliminating discriminatory policies and practices once prevalent in higher educational institutions.is reviewed. Of substantial distinction have been Committee W's efforts to seek economic parity and financial equity for academic women.

Greenfield, E. From equal to equivalent pay: Salary discrimination in academia. *Journal of Law and Education,* 1977, *6*(1), 41–62.

Examines the federal statutes barring sex discrimination in employment and argues that the work of any two professors is comparable but not equal. Suggests using regression analysis to prove salary discrimination and discusses the legal justification for adopting regression analysis and the standard of comparable pay for comparable work.

Kimmel, E.B. *The status of faculty women: A method for documentation and correction of salary and rank inequities due to sex.* [ERIC ED 074996]

> It is an increasingly well-documented fact that women in American universities suffer from sex discrimination. Recent federal legislation makes it legally as well as morally imperative that employment policies in higher education afford equal opportunity to women. This document presents a description of a method utilized at the University of South Florida to find specific corrective measures to eliminate existing and future sex discrimination. It was first used for documentation purposes and subsequently for corrective ones.

Lussier, V.L. Academic collective bargaining: Panacea or palliative for women and minorities? *Labor Law Journal*, 1976, *27*(9), 565–572.

> "This article examines areas in which collective bargaining has aided or reinforced affirmative action goals and areas in which the principles of affirmative action and collective bargaining potentially conflict with ont another." The article is based upon consultation with faculty and administrators involved in collective bargaining at seventeen institutions, and upon review of the collective bargaining contracts for those institutions. Nondiscrimination, equal pay and salary inequity, seniority, tenure, and arbitration are covered.

Mitchell, J.M. & Starr, R.R. A regional approach for analyzing the recruitment of academic women. *American Behavioral Scientist*, 1971, *15*(2), 183–205.

> Findings and discussion of a regional study on women vis-a-vis recruitment processes, placement systems, employment conditions, and opportunities for professional performance.

Peden, I.C. & Sloan, M.E. Faculty women: Strategies for the future. *IEEE Transactions on Education*, 1975, *E-18*(1), 57–65.

> A unique assessment of women engineering educators. Included in this examination are the status and rank of women academic enigeers, and their position vis-a-vis mobility into university administration. Strategies for future amelioration are also discussed.

Reagan, B.B. & Maynard. B.J. Sex discrimination in universities — approach through internal labor market analysis. *AAUP Bulletin*, 1974, *60*(1), 13–21.

> Discussion of a study at Southern Methodist University which used internal labor market analysis to (1) determine average salary differentials due to sex

discrimination, and (2) to identify individual cases of sex-based salary differentials. The analytic method is discussed at length, and its usefulness for other institutions is emphasized.

Reuben, E. & Hoffmann, L. (Eds.) *Unladylike and unprofessional: Academic women and academic unions.* New York. Modern Language Association of America, 1975. [ERIC ED 104270]

This pamphlet deals with the professional concerns of academic women. Topics of articles cover: definition of terms in collective bargaining; faculty women at the bargaining table; women faculty and the union at Oakland University; folk wisdom of collective bargaining in Michigan; maintaining balance in a collective agreement; unions, poltics, and reality; peer judgment and the rule of confidentiality; advantages and disadvantages of women in the union; a history of the CUNY women's movement; and reflections about women and faculty unions.

Sandler, B. Women on the campus and collective bargaining: It doesn't have to hurt to be a woman in labor. *Journal of the College and University Personnel Association*, 1974, *25*(2), 82–89.

Discusses how the women's movement and campus collective bargaining can interrelate by giving women a new weapon to use in their struggle to end discrimination on campus.

Schmeller, K.R. Collective bargaining and women in higher education. *College and University Journal*, 1973, *12*(3), 34–36.

The president of Queensborough Community College (CUNY) discusses collective bargaining and contractual agreements as "instruments of affirmative and reformist action." Collective bargaining "can provide opportunities for positive, joint efforts, to eliminte sexual and other forms of discrimination."

Shapley, D. University women's rights: Whose feet are dragging? *Science*, 1972, *175*(4018), 151–154.

Surveys the progress made by the Department of Health, Education, and Welfare in enforcing equal opportunities for the employment of women in university research projects sponsored by federal funds. Concludes that contract compliance is proving a clumsy mechanism for women's groups anxious to make rapid changes at their universities.

Smith, G.M. Faculty women at the bargaining table. *AAUP Bulletin,* 1973, *59*(4), 402–406.

> A case history of faculty women at the bargaining table, preceded by synopses of three, mutually reinforcing conditions that "make this the best time in history for women at the bargaining table": the advent of collective bargaining in academe, the growth of feminist organizations, and federal antidiscrimination laws.

Theodore, A. *Academic women in protest.* Expanded version of a paper presented at the Annual Meeting of the Society for the Study of Social Problems, New York, August 25, 1973. [ERIC ED 091989]

> This paper is an exploratory inquiry into some aspects of protest for sex equality by academic women. The analysis is based on published and unpublished information on sex discrimination in academia, as well as on a sample of 65 cases of academic women obtained from a pilot survey. Part II emphasizes patterns of response to sex discrimination including sensitizing academics, using of "regular" channels, confrontation, and activism outside academia. Part III reviews the effects of protest on the individual and on the institution. Part IV analyzes the accomplishments and failures derived from protesting women's strategems. Part V, an overview of future response to the women's movement, discusses the corrective actions that should be taken by government agencies and professional associations as well as needed academic reforms.

Tidball, M.E. & Kistiakowsky, V. Baccalaureate origins of American scientists and scholars. *Science,* 1976, *193*(4254), 646–652.

> This study characterizes colleges and universities with respect to their advancement of the status of women. Insitutional productivity was measured by both the absolute number and percentage of its graduates of each sex who went on to earn the doctorate. Both measures of productivity were also assessed with respect to the decades when the baccalaureates were granted and the fields of doctoral study pursued by the degree recipient. The environment found to be most productive of women who eventually received doctorates was an environment where large numbers of were present, where there was a long and continuous history of women graduates who obtained doctorates, and where strong academic preparation in several fields was available. This was different from the most productive environment for men doctorates.

Travis, T.G. Affirmative action on campus: How firm the foundation? *The Journal of the National Association for Women Deans, Administrators, and Counselors*, 1976, *39*(2): 50–57.

> Discusses the impact of the Holmes memorandum on affirmative action in educational institutions.

Wasserman, E., Lewin, A.Y. & Bleiweis, L.H. (Eds.). *Women in academia - equal opportunities*. New York: Praeger, 1975.

> Focuses on the power balance existing in universities in which academic departments often have more power than central administrations in the areas of staffing promotion, tenure, and salaries. Proposes affirmative organizational structures to assure equal opportunity without compromising the academic independence of departments.

Women in the Disciplines

Astin, H.S. Employment and career status of women psychologists. *American Psychologist,* 1972, *27*(5), 371–381.

> Astin's study concludes that even when women hold doctorates from top institutions or publish equivalently with their male counterparts, they have a harder time finding positions, are paid less, and receive less recognition in the form of high rank and tenure.

Bruce, J.D. The search for women faculty members. *IEEE Transactions on Education,* 1975, *E-18*(1), 53–57.

> Discusses the statistics on women faculty in engineering, why they have a lower representation than in the corresponding student body, and what changes might be made in the future. Not only are women engineering doctorates in extremely short supply, but engineering departments are currently able to accept 25% more students without new faculty.

Crawford, M.C., Moody, J.B., & Tullis, J. Women in academia - students and professors, *Geology,* 1977, *5*(8), 502–503.

> This article, derived from a symposium entitled Women and Careers in geoscience, provides a brief overview of the participation and status of women in academic careers in the geosceinces: both student and professional careers. Good statistics, and some discussion of the reasons for the current state-of-the-art are offered.

Deutrich, M.E. Women in archives - a summary report of the Committee on the Status of Women in the Archival Profession. *The American Archivist,* 1975, *38*(1), 43–46.

> Documents discrimination in the archival field. [See also: Deutrich, M.E. Women in archives — Ms. vs. Mr. Archivist. *The American Archivist,* 1973, *36*(2), 171–182.rb

Fields, R. The status of women in psychology. *International Journal of Group Tensions*, 1974, *4*(1), 93–121.

> This article is a valuable source of information on the status of women in all major divisions of the field of psychology (industrial, engineering, consumer, etc.). The fundamental finding is that life patterns of women psychologists contain circumstances which "mandate a different process of career development, extend to and from a discriminatory reward system, and indicate limited access to power and decision-making..."

Flora, C.B. Women in rural sociology. *Rural Sociology*, 1972, *37*, 454–461.

> Good survey of the status of women in rural sociology, including women as students in the field and support for female graduate study. Data is mostly from late 1960's and early 1970's, but some tables extend back as far as the 1930's.

Green, A.A. Women on the chemistry faculties of institutions granting the Ph.D. in chemistry. Washington, D.C.: American Chemical Society, 1976. [ERIC ED 134120]

> The 1973 study by the women chemists committee is updated for the 1974–1975 academic year. Only professors, associate professors, and assistant professors are included, since lecturers, instructors, and others are not considered full-time appointees or holders of permanent positions. The revision shows that some Chemistry departments have added women to their faculties for the first time since the 1973 report. But of the large departments with over 30 faculty members and no women in 1973, only three of 26 have added women faculty members.

Hughes, H.M. (Ed.) *The status of women in sociology 1968–1972*. A report to the American Sociological Association of the Ad Hoc Committee on the Status of Women in the Profession. Washington, D.C.: American Sociological Association, 1973.

> Excellent statistical profiles of women in sociology 1968–1972 (Chapter 1), followed by informative analyses of women graduate students in sociology (Chapter 2), women faculty, and women's participation in American Sociological Association and in professional publications. Concluding chapters provide "food for thought" to women graduate stuents and a list of recommendations.

La Sorte, M.A. Sex differences in salary among academic sociology teachers. *American Sociologist*, 1971, *6*, 304–307.

> Documents a salary gap between male and female sociologists, but labels as

"untenable any suggestion that there is a widespread, institutionalized policy purposefully structured to discriminate on the basis of one's gender."

Lewin, A.Y. & Duchan, L. Women in academia. *Science,* 1971, *173*, 892–895.

A study of hiring decisions in 111 graduate departments of physical sciences (62% response from 179). Average male applicants were preferred over average female applicants for a hypothetical faculty position, but superior women were recognized. In the latter case, however, a considerable volume of unsollicited commentary was received by the researchers expressing concern about the applicant's husband, children, and her compatibility with existing department members.

Liebman, J.S. Women in engineering at the University of Illinois in Urbana-Champaign. *IEEE Transactions on Education,* 1975, *E-18*(1), 47–49.

The participation of women as students and as faculty members in the College of Engineering at the University of Illinois at Urbana-Champaign is examined in this paper.

Luchins, E.H. *Women in mathematics: Problems of orientation and reorientation. Final Report.* Troy, N.Y.: Rensselaer Polytechnic Institute, 1976. [ERIC ED 129634]

This problem-assessment study sought answers to the problems of why there are relatively few women in mathematics, what encouraged or discouraged contemporary women mathematicians, and what can be done to attract more women to the mathematical sciences. A questionnaire was developed and sent to members of the Association for Women in Mathematics (AWM). This document contains an analysis of the responses to the questionnaire, career patterns and interests, AWM respondents' present status, international problems, and varied attempts at explanations.

Montanelli, R.G., Jr. & Mamrak, S.A. The status of women and minorities in academic computer science. *Communciations of the ACM,* 1976, *19*(10), 578–581.

Results of an extensive survey concerning women and minorities in computer science between 1971–1975. Special recruitment programs are needed for both degree programs and employment.

Patterson, M. Alice in wonderland: A study of women faculty in graduate departments of sociology. *American Sociologist,* 1971, *6*, 226–234.

Women are systematically excluded from two organizational rewards that most influence an individual's prestige within the discipline: membership in high-ranking departments and high rank in almost all departments.

Perkins, J.A. Women in the modern languages. *Bulletin of the Association of Departments of Foreign Languages* (Special joint issue with Bulletin of the Association of Departments of English, Number 50, September 1976), 1976, *8*(1), 44–48.

The position of women is compared to that of men in the college teaching profession, including the percentages they comprise, salary differences, and factors affecting tenure.

Reagan, B.B. Report of the committee on the status of women in the economics profession. *The American Economic Review,* 1975, *65*, 490–501.

Excellent source of statistics on women in economics; up to date and well presented.

Rossi, A.S. Status of women in graduate departments of sociology. *American Sociologist,* 1970, *5*, 1–12.

Results of a survey on the status of academic women (students, faculty, research personnel) in graduate departments of sociology from 1968 to 1969. Disheartening but good statistics.

Standley, K. and others. Women in architecture. *Journal of Architectural Education,* 1974, *27*(4), 78–82.

Stems from a series of interviews and questionnaires completed by 27 female architects. Covers the sex-typing of a profession and a case study of a woman architect.

Stead, B.A. *Women management faculty: An empirical look at their status.* Houston, TX: University of Texas, 1975. [ERIC ED 122693]

Eighty-one (46%) useable questionnaires were returned. The conclusions of this study were: (1) 25 percent of female academy members are not receiving raises and promotion at the time they met criteria; (2) half the female academy members may be considered a talent pool for administrative openings since they have strong self-concepts about their administrative ability and are interested in these positions; (3) a significant number of female academy members are not job hunting; (4) some benefits have been received by female academy members from the women's movement; (5) over a third of female academy members may be considered a talent pool for industry; (6) female students of academy members are still having problems getting jobs;

(7) over half the sample is concentrated in the lower salary ranges, yet over half the sample is found in the higher age range; and (8) the above conclusions coupled with lack of free-and-open communication by administrators and perceived attitudes toward women by both chairmen and deans seem to indicate a lack of affirmative action.

Vetter, B.M. Women in the natural sciences. *Signs,* 1976, *1*(3), 713–720.

Reviews the status of women in the natural sciences. Includes statistics on doctorates earned by women, (also B.S. and M.S. degrees), distribution of these in the field, and salary. Women in the natural sciences have approximately the same status as they did in 1970.

Watkins, B. Women and history. *Change,* 1974, *6*(4), 17–20.

The women's movement has radically affected the teaching and writing of history, but women historians still do not have employment equality in their profession.

White, B.E. *Women's Caucus of the College Art Association survey of the status of women in 164 art departments in accredited institutions of higher education.* New York: College Art Association, 1973 [ERIC ED 074901]

This document presents statistical data on the status of women in full-time teaching positions in 164 college and university art departments. The percentage of women at various faculty ranks decreases steadily from instructor to full professor. Necessarily the opposite is true for men. The data do not provide an answer to why "the higher, the fewer" relationship holds so pervasively. However, they do indicate that in those departments that have Ph.D.'s on their faculties, the percentage of women with Ph.D.'s exceeds the percentage of men by almost 25%. Hence, although women are concentrated at the lower ranks, they may be more highly trained on the average than their male colleagues.

Wilcox, T. The lot of the woman: A report on the national survey of undergraduate English programs. *Bulletin of the Association of Departments of English,* 1970, *25*, 53–59. *lbERIC ED 044090*rb

There is widespread belief that those in charge of selecting and promoting college teachers of English discriminate against women, either deliberately or unwittingly. Though the proportion of women who have risen to the upper ranks is considerably smaller than the proportion of men, this may be due less to discrimination than to the fact that more women than men drop out of the profession or fail to pursue their professional career with full energy and dedication.

Wolfe, J.C., DeFleur, M.C. & Slocum, W.E. Sex discrimination in hiring practices of graduate sociology departments: Myths and realities. *American Sociologist,* 1973, *8*(4), 159–168.

> Reviews existing studies on the topic and critiques their lack of control for those intervening variables that determine career success and advancement for both sexes, and presents findings from a study in which appropriate controls were applied. Prejudicial staffing procedures are shown to be relatively unimportant compared with the real problem of insufficient female recruits to graduate work in sociology, and the subsequent dearth of qualified female applicants for faculty positions.

Women's toehold on chemistry faculties still just that. *Chemical and Engineering News,* 1976, *54*(48), 47–48.

> Discusses statistics resulting from a report on female professors, associate professors, and assistant professors on the faculties of Ph.D. granting chemistry departments during the year 1974–1975.

Wood, M.A. *Profile of the woman journalism teacher in the two-year college.* Paper presented to the Ad Hoc Committee on the Status of Women in Journalism Education, Association for Education in Journalism, Ottawa, Canada, August 18, 1975. [ERIC ED 129346]

> This paper reports the results of a 1975 survey of 169 female Journalism instructors in community colleges, conducted for the purpose of developing a demographic profile and to gather information about professional journalism and teaching experience relative to salary and other job-related topics. Of those surveyed, 54 usable responses were obtained.

Zelinsky, W. Women in geography - a brief factual account. *Professional Geographer,* 1973, *25*(2), 151–165.

> A comprehensive, concise, factual account of women in academic geography at the graduate and professional levels. Good tables, good statistics, and good bibliography.

Zuckerman, H. & Cole, J.R. Women in American science. *Minerva,* 1975, *13*(1), 84–102.

> The small numbers of women in the physical and biological sciences and the other learned professions in the United States result from early and cumulative discrepancies in the extent and character of educational attainment.

Women Academics vs. Men Academics: Traits, States, and Productivity

Blackstone, T. & Fulton, O. Men and women academics: An Anglo-American comparison of subject choices and research activity. *Higher Education,* 1974, *3*(2), 119–140.

> Women in both the U.S. and the U.K. are concentrated in the humanities and are virtually absent from the applied sciences; in both countries women are a small minority across all subject areas stuided. The polarization between men and women is greater in the U.S.: most severe in the humanities and least severe in the social and applied sciences. American women faculty were found to teach more than their male counterparts, whereas the converse was true in Britain (except in the social sciences). Includes a discussion of causes of the noted differences.

Eckert, R. Academic women revisited. *Liberal Education,* 1971, *57*(4), 479–87.

> This is the second study comparing women and men professors in Minnesota. It is one of very few studies that has taken a statewide perspective and that has involved longitudinal data from the 1959 study.

Farmer, H.S. Why women contribute less to the arts, sciences, and humanities. Paper presented at the annual meeting of the American Educational Research Association, San Francisco, California, April 19–23, 1976. [ERIC ED 123178]

> Women do not contribute to the arts, sciences, and humanities commensurately with their talents and potential nor in proportion to the opportunities available to them. This study investigated variables or combinations of variables which best predict lower achievement and career motivation in women: self-esteem, fear of success, vicarious achievement ethic, home-career conflict, work-discrimination beliefs, sex-role orientation, risk-taking behavior, social structure, and perception of parents.

Ferber, M.A. & Loeb, J.W. Performance, rewards, and perceptions of sex discrimination among male and female faculty. *American Journal of Sociology,* 1973, *78*(4), 995–1002.

> "Some correlates of productivity and reward among male and female faculty members are investigated. Marital and parental status is related to productivity, salary, and rank for men and women. In addition, productivity and reward of men and women are related to the percent of the department which is female." [taken from Sociological Abstracts No. 74G7286]

Groth, N.J. Success and creativity in male and female professors. *The Gifted Child Quarterly,* 1975, *19*(4), 328–335.

> A good literature review on creativity of men and women academics. Women are shown to fall behind men in creative endeavors such as research publications and publication of books. Biological correlates are inadequately supported as yet, and cultural correlates concentrate on sex-role stereotyping. The paper proposes alternate explanatory possibilities.

Hamovitch, W. & Morgenstern, R.D. Children and the productivity of academic women. *Journal of Higher Education,* 1977, *48*(6), 633–645.

> A statistical examination of the relationship between child rearing and scholarly productivity among academic women. Findings showed that women publish "somewhat less" than men, but that child-rearing does not appear relevant to the number of publications of academic women. Women who are bringing up children also have equal likelihood with men of being considered outstanding by their peers.

Harlan, A. et al. *Sex, productivity, and reward in academe.* Paper presented at the 82nd Annual Meeting of the American Psychological Association, New Orleans, Louisiana, August 1974. [ERIC ED 097619]

> This study attempts to utilize more refined measures of rewards and productivity than have been employed in past research in an effort to determine whether differences in rewards offered to men and women exist, and if they do, whether such differences can be explained in terms of differing rates of productivity.

Knudsin, R.B. (Ed.);Successful women in the sciences: An analysis of determinants. *Annals of the New York Academy of Sciences,* 1973, *208*, entire volume.

> This volume is a report of a conference on the theme expressed in the title. Most pieces are non-research, but the volume as a whole provides a rich source of information on women scientists as academics, as professionals, and as women. Contributors include Matina Horner, Cynthia Epstein, and Patricia Albjerg Graham.

Pinson, C.B. & Caffrey, B. Self-acceptance in females as a function of academic achievement. *Psychological Reports,* 1976, *38*(3), 853–854.

> This study was intended to evaluate the hypothesis that interaction with fellow professionals leads to heightened self-esteem in women in science. The hypothesis was upheld.

Tidball, M.E. Of men and research: The dominant themes in American higher education include neither teaching nor women. *Journal of Higher Education*, 1976, *47*(4), 373–89.

A survey of teaching faculty conducted by the American Council of Education (ACE) revealed that most college and university environments are relatively nonsupportive of women faculty and students, and that men faculty subscribe to the institution's research image for self esteem while women utilize other value systems to define success.

Tidball, M.E. Perspective on academic women and affirmative action. *Educational Record*, 1973, *54*(2), 130–135.

A study of 1500 career-successful women and their collegiate origins. The tendency was for high achievers to have graduated from women's colleges where twice as many faculty members are women as in all other institutions. The author's conclusion is that "the development of young women of talent into career-successful adults is directly proportional to the number of role models to whom they have access."

Tidball, M.E. The search for talented women. *Change*, 1974, *6*(4), 51–52.

This article reports on a study that sought to learn who women achievers are, what educational background characteristics they share, and what the relationship is between marriage and career success. The sample was a random 2% of all college graduates listed in *Who's Who of American Women, 1966–71*. The most striking commonality among these women was that they attended women's colleges, and specifically that the higher the female faculty/female student ratio was, the greater was the number of female graduates who achieve.

Wiles, M.M. *Cross-referencing the professorship, male induction and female sexuality models: An inherent "inappropriateness" referrent, 1976.* [*ERIC ED 123750*]

Appropriateness for any particular organization role involves a calculation of identifiable expectations. The induction phase of new members identifies a set of role expectations. Unobtrusive but obvious "other" expectations play a large part in determining the appropriateness of both role and induction in organizations. This paper discusses the unconventional expectations associated with the label "feminine" as it affects role referrents of professorship within higher education. It is hypothesized that the present lack of consistent expectations for female faculty has created role confusion that cannot be alleviated by manipulation of traditional bureaucratic, male, or induction role expectations. Specifically, cross-referencing the conventional classifications of university professional, male induction, and female sexuality reveals two types of role inappropriateness for the female professor: (1) that in direct conflict with the traditional male induction model, and/or (2) a professor role that has no "correct" sexuality referrent.

General Studies

Epstein, C.R. *Woman's place,* Berkeley, CA: University of California Press, 1970.

    Discusses female socialization and reconciliation to the roles of women. Includes studies on the barriers for women's achieving professional status. The thrust of the book is directed toward the examination of the attitudes which have hindered advancement of women.

Freeman, B.F. Faculty women in the American university: Up the down staircase. *Higher Education,* 1977, 6(2), 165–188.

    This article has three major components: (1) a comparison of the status of academic women and men at the most prestigous U.S. institutions; (2) an account of women's organization within academic professional organizations, (3) an assessment of the impact of such organizations on government policy. Future prospects for women, given current conditions of declining birthrate, economic instability, and economic stringency within higher education, is also considered.

Hollander, H.E., Penney, S., & Haines, J.R. (Eds.). Women in the university. In *Women: Their future in the university and the community.* Albany, NY: Higher Education Management Services of the New York State Education Department, 1974.

    The section of this conference report on "Women in the University" contains three relevant discussions of affirmative action: Commissioner Nyquist reviews the situation in New York State; Marilyn Gittel presents the brief for too much rhetoric and not enough concrete progress; and Esther Kronovet presents the results of a study on community college affirmative action.

Howard, S. *But we will persist.* Washington, D.C.: AAUW, 1978.

    Reports the results of a survey of institutions concerning the status of academic women. Provides the best overall statistics for the decade. [See also Oltman, R. for an earlier version of the study.]

Kilson, M. The status of women in higher education, *Signs: Journal of Women in Culture and Society.* 1976, *1*(4), 935–942.

> Declining population and restrictive economy mean that while the percentage of women filling academic positions may remain constant or increase, actual numbers will decline. This is taken as a possible erosion of ground gained to date. An excellent review of current review and opinion.

Krenkel, N. *An informational paper on activities of women's committees in a sample of professional associations.* Washington, D.C.: American Educational Research Association. [ERIC ED 112731]

> The data compiled in this study represent the responses of professional associations regarding the activities of women's committees.

Mackay, M. *Status of women committee: Faculty report.* Tampa, Fla.: AAUP, 1970. [ERIC ED 049698]

> This report on the status of women summarized data from six sources. The report begins with a brief review of the reasons for an AAUP report on the status of women at the State University system of Florida, the main one of which is a charge of sex discrimination against the whole state university system.

Oltman, R.M. *Campus 1970. Where do women stand?* Research report on a survey of women in academe. Washington, D.C.: AAUW, 1970. [ERIC ED 046366]

> This report describes the results of a questionnaire which was sent to the presidents of 750 colleges and universities which hold institutional membership in the AAUW; 454 of these responded. The purpose of the questionnaire was to evaluate the activities of women and the extent to which they were involved in the university as students, administrators, faculty, and trustees. Specifically, an effort was made to determine the participation of women in decision making; personnel policies affecting hiring, promotion, maternity leave, and nepotism; special programs designed for mature women students; utilization of women's abilities in major offices and committees, as department heads, principal administrators and trustees; and general attitudes of administration regarding women.

Percentage of women professors is four times national average in women's college survey. Washington, D.C.: Women's College Coalition, 1976. [ERIC ED 126791]

> An in-depth survey of women's colleges (27 independent private, 20 church-related, and two public) sought information in such areas as curricu-

lum, continuing education, athletics, career support services, and the presence of women in teaching, administrative, and board positions. The percentage of women faculty members at women's colleges is two-and one-half times the national average for all institutions of higher education, and the percentage of women with the rank of full professor in the women's colleges is more than four times the national average. Other key findings are that: (1) financial aid for the continuing education student is available at nearly 75% of the colleges; (2) more than 50% of the responing colleges indicate their fastest growing majors to be business administration, biology, economics, or nursing; (3) 96 percent of the responding colleges have courses on women in their curriculum; and (4) there is intercollegiate athletic competition at more than 90% of the responding colleges, with an average of five intercollegiate sports at each college. Athletic scholarships are offered by 12 percent.

The status of women faculty and administrators in higher educational institutions, 1971–1972. NEA Research Memo No. 1973–7. Washington, D.C.: National Educational Association, 1973, pp. 1–2.

This research memo provides a brief report of the status of women faculty and administrators in higher education based on three types of information collected in the NEA Research biennial study of salaries in higher education in 1971–72. In addition to summarizing faculty salaries by sex, this memo reports the tenure status of faculty and reviews the number of persons and their salaries in administrative positions in higher education by sex.

Theodore, A. *The professional woman.* New York: Schenckman Publishing Co., 1971.

An especially rich compendium of works on women professionals. Includes sections on trends and prospects (I), the sexual structure of professions (II), cultural definitions of the female professional (III), career choice processes (IV), adult socialization and career commitment (V), career patterns and marriage (VI); the marginal professional (VII); and female professionalism and social change (VIII). Each section contains items specifically pertinning to undergraduates, graduates, and faculty.

Vetter, B.M. & Babco, E.L. *Professional women and minorities. A manpower resources service.* Washington, D.C.: Scientific Manpower Commission, May 1975. [ERIC ED 109978]

This document was prepared to assist those persons or groups seeking data on the participation and availability of women and/or minorities in those professional areas generally requiring formal education to at least the baccalaureate level. More than 100 data sources were used to provide information for this compilation including materials from government agencies, professional associations, and women's and/or minority groups and caucuses.

What is this thing called coeducation? *Mount Holyoke Alumnae Quarterly,* 1972, 55(4), 241–52.

This article reviews statistics on coeducation in the major private colleges and universities, especially the pertinent information on the sex ratios of the faculties.

Pingree, S. & Butler-Paisley, M. *Attitudes toward hiring a professional couple: Results of a recent survey.* Paper presented at the Symposium on Academic/Professional Women in Communication and Related Fields, International Communication Association, New Orleans, Louisiana, April 1974. [ERIC ED 095738].

A questionnaire sent to the chairperson of either the psychology or the sociology department of all colleges and universities in the United States explored the extent and nature of attitudes about hiring Ph.D. couples in the same department. A total of 2,027 colleges and universities comprised the sample group, however, only 16 percent (329) returned the questionnaire. Results indicate that administrators who would oppose hiring a husband-wife team in the same department are in the minority, and that antinepotism policies and attitudes are no longer prevalent. The 33 percent of department chairpersons who did respond in the bottom third of the scale are a sizable minority. It is possible that nearly a third of the time the Ph.D. couple will be greeted with a chairperson who at least actively opposes their candidacy for two positions in her/his department. Advantages and disadvantages to both the department and to the couple are indicated.

Weissman, M.M. and others. The faculty wife: Her academic interests and qualifications. *AAUP Bulletin,* 1972, 58(3), 287–292.

Presents the results of a survey of 262 faculty wives and 20 women faculty at Yale. A one-of-a-kind study in terms of its focus on the untapped resources available to higher education of women in the local community.

CHAPTER SEVEN

Bibliographies and Demographic Studies

Introduction

Chapter VII is intended as a "holding" category under which we have grouped three otherwise unrelated categories. The first of these is a collection of bibliographical works, the second a collection of demographic studies, and the third an unannotated list of regionally delimited or campus reports.

There are several excellent annotated bibliographical works available for those pursuing research topics on academic women. Included here are bibliographies covering a broad range of topical foci, with citations generally dating within the last ten to fifteen years. One bibliography has been included specifically for the purpose of covering pre-1970 material since our own selection of references begins at about 1970.

The demographic studies generally comprise data too broad to fit into one of the other more specific chapters. Typically, they cover women students, faculty and administrators rather than only one of these groups and for this reason they have been clustered generically rather than topically.

Bibliographies

Astin, H.S., Suniewick, N. & Dweck, S. *Women: A bibliography on their education and careers*. New York: Behavioral Publications Inc., 1971 and 1974.

Excellent annotated bibliography of mostly empirical studies with an introductory overview of the findings and substantive abstracts of the 352 entires.

Barabas, J. *Women: Their educational and career roles. An annotated bibliography of selected ERIC references*. ERIC-IRCD Urban Disadvantaged Series, Number 31. New York: Columbia University: ERIC Clearinghouse on the Urban Disadvantaged, August 1972. [ERIC ED 067423]

This annotated bibliography has been prepared to deal with the issue of women as a group whose realistic and creative contributions have often been hindered by traditional employment patterns and social institutions. The listing encompasses document citations in *Research in Education* from November 1966 through December 1971, and journal citations in *Current Index to Journals in Education* from January 1969 through December 1971. Much of the literature cited is research oriented, and is divided into seven sections: women in the society, counseling women, women in academia (as students), continuing education for women, career choice and development for women, and women in the world of work.

Friedman, B. (Ed.). *Women's work and women's studies: 1973–1974*. Barnard College Women's Center, 1975.

This is a comprehensive bibliography (third edition) of books, articles, papers, pamphlets, and research on women published or in progress in 1973–1974. Section E3 covers college and continuing education; Section E4 covers graduate and professional school; and Section J2 deals with legal status vis-a-vis employment.

Harmon, L. *Status of women in higher education: 1963–1972. A selective bibliography*. Ames, Iowa: Iowa State University, 1972. [ERIC ED 070384]

A selective annotated bibliography concerning women and their status in higher education.

Mills, G.H. [Compiler] *Equal rights for women in education. Seminar 6, a bibliography*. Denver, Colorado: Education Comission of the States, 1973. Presented at the Annual Meeting of the Education Commission of the States (June 20–22, 1974). [ERIC ED 102439]

This is a selected bibliography covering a subject which was under consideration at the seventh annual meeting of the Education Commission of the States in 1973. Articles listed under the overall topic of equal rights for women cover the following subjects: (1) affirmative action, (2) continuing education and counseling of women, (3) employment profiles and opportunities, (4) manpower research, (5) sex discrimination, (6) women's studies, and (7) the status of women in higher education.

Women in higher education: A selected bibliography, Pennsylvania State Library-Harrisburg. General Library Bureau. 1975.

Emphasizes current material of use to affirmative action officers in institutions of higher education.

Robinson, L.H. *Institutional analysis of sex discrimination: A review and annotated bibliography.* Washington, D.C.: ERIC Clearinghouse on Higher Education, 1973. [ERIC ED 076176]

Several conditions contribute to the need for information about women's standing in the academic community. Women's groups and individuals continue to file complaints of sex discrimination against colleges and universities with federal agencies having enforcement responsibilities in this area. In addition, civil suits have arisen, and institutions are faced with developing affirmative action plans that include women in their focus. While some schools have already completed one or more studies of the status of women on campus, others have yet to undertake this task. This report is designed for those embarking on such studies in the near future. The bibliography was designed to facilitate information gathering and utilization in three ways: to aid cross comparisons between institutions: to help locate useful analytical approaches; and to highlight the variety of concerns that have received attention.

Westervelt, E.M. & Fixter, D. *Women's higher and continuing education: An annotated bibliography with selected references on related aspects of women's lives.* N.J.: College Entrance Examination Board, 1971. [ERIC ED 053375]

This document is principally an annotated bibliography of works dealing with women in higher education. A total of 290 annotations are included. Twenty additional annotations are contained concerning related aspects of women's lives. [N.B.: Especially good for pre-1970 citations, not included the present bibliography.]

Demographic Studies

A guide to sources of data on women and women workers for the United States and for regions, states, and local areas. Washington, D.C.: Department of Labor Women's Bureau, 1972. [ERIC ED 067035]

This document presents a list of suggested source material to aid employers and other interested persons in acquiring statistical data needed in the development of programs for affirmative action for women wokers. This listing identifies selected publications currently available or soon to be published on persons by sex, race, educational attainment, labor force participation, occupation, and industry. Availability of data by region, state, standard metropolitan statistical area, or other area is designated.

A look at women in education: Issues and answers for HEW. Report of the Commissioner's Task Force on the Impact of Office of Education Programs on Women. Washington, D.C.: United States Office of Education, 1972. [ERIC ED 091957]

This report examines sex discrimination in institutions of higher education and its implications for all Office of Education programs. Part I presents an overview of sex discrimination in education, and Part II describes the relationship between the federal education agencies and the pervasive sex discrimination documented in Part I. Chapter I outlines existing discrimination in health, education, and welfare programs and necessary steps to carry out a legal mandate to end discrimination in federal education programs. Chapter II presents a plan for creative federal leadership in fulfilling the spirit of the law against sex discrimination.

Berkowitz, T., Mangi, J., Williamson, J. (Eds.). *Who's who and where in women's studies.* Old Westbury, New York: Feminist Press, 1974.

A reference work listing faculty who have taught women's studies courses, the course titles, and the departments and institutions where such courses have been offered. The faculty listing in particular may be of use since most professors listed are themselves women academics.

Blitz, R.C. Women in the professions, 1870-1970. *Monthly Labor Review,* 1971, 97, 34–39.

The proportion of women occupying professional positions has diminished steadily since 1930; this decrease has occurred as the distribution of jobs traditionally filled by women and men has gradually changed to favor the latter.

Carnegie Commission on Higher Education. *Opportunities for women in higher education: Their current participation, prospects for the future, and recommendations for future action.* N.Y.: McGraw-Hill, 1973.

> An excellent statistical report on women and discrimination in all levels of university life: student, faculty and administration. Extensive bibliography.

Chmaj, B.E. Image, myth and beyond. *American Women and American Studies,* Vol. 2, 1972. [ERIC ED 121192]

> The status of American women and women's studies are described. Part 1 of the report covers the status of women in universities and the professions. Part 2, on courses and programs, deals with course syllabi and commentary, programs of women's studies courses at specific institutions, continuing education programs, and a women's history research center. Images and myths concerning colleges and women are examined in Part 3. Specific issues addressed include: official positions toward women, the women's liberation movement, female instructors, the concept of women in literature, women in American history, film stereotypes, stereotypes in comic books, and images of women in Nineteenth and Twentieth Century art.

Harris, A.S. The second sex in academe. *AAUP Bulletin,* 1970, 56(3), 283–295.

> A statistically-based discussion of discrimination against women in academe. Includes students, faculty, administrators, the "employment grapevine," *de facto* versus *de jure* sexual discrimination. Good further bibliography of items from late 1960's and 1970.

Sexton, P. *Women in education.* Phi Delta Kappa Education Foundation, 1976.

> A rich source of descriptive statistics on academic women is available in the appendix of this volume. A brief chapter on academic women is also included, and treats questions of their status in higher education.

Institutional and Geographically Delimited Studies

California

Bratfisch, V. and others. *A report on the status of women at the California State College at Fullerton.* June 1970. [ERIC ED 045044]
Fisher, K.M. *Report of the Task Force on the State of Women at the University of California, Davis.* June 1972. [ERIC ED 074979]
Stanford University School of Medicine. *Report of the professional women of Stanford Medical School.* December, 1969. [ERIC ED 067983]
Stark, N. and others. *of Women at UCLA.* June 1972. [ERIC ED 071635]
University of California, Berkeley. *Report of the Subcommittee on the Status of Academic Women on the Berkeley Campus.* May 1970. [ERIC ED 042413]
University of California, Santa Cruz. *Report of the Special Committee on the Status of Women at USC.* October 1971. [ERIC ED 080069]

Canada

Payton, L.C. *The status of women in the Ontario Universities.* June, 1975. [ERIC ED 111324]

Colorado

AAUP (Denver). *Study of faculty women at the University of Denver.* April, 1970. [ERIC ED 081312]
Minturn, L. *Inequities in salary payments to faculty women.* (University of Colorado at Boulder) May, 1970. [ERIC ED 045045]

Connecticut

Connecticut Education Association. *Fifty-one percent minority. Connecticut Conference on the Status of Women.* August 1972. [ERIC ED 074958]
Weitzman, L. and others. *Women on the Yale faculty.* March, 1971. [ERIC ED 056636]
Yale University. *A Report to the president from the Committee on the Status of Professional Women at Yale.* May, 1971. [ERIC ED 052701]

Florida

Mackay, M. *Status of Women Committee: Faculty Report.* Tampa, Fla.: AAUP, 1970. [ERIC ED 049688]

New York

Babey-Brooke, M. & Amber, R.B. *Discrimination against women in higher education. A 15 year survey.* July, 1970. [ERIC ED 044089]

City University of New York. *Affirmative action at CUNY.* November, 1971. [ERIC ED 080049]

City University of New York, Brooklyn College. *Chancellor's Advisory Committee on the State of Women at CUNY.* September, 1972. [ERIC ED 071560]

City University of New York. *The status of women at the City University of New York: A report to the chancellor.* December, 1972. [ERIC ED 081347]

Francis, B. *The status of women at Cornell.* 1970. [ERIC ED 044095]

Delaware

Dahl, K.H. *Report on women at the University of Delaware.* 1971. [ERIC ED 056631]

Illinois

Ferber, M. & Leob, J. *Rank, pay, and representation of women on the faculty at the Urbana-Champaign campus of the University of Illinois.* November, 1970. [ERIC ED 045011]

Illinois State University (Normal). *The status of women faculty at Illinois State University, 1970–1971.* 1971. [ERIC ED 058836]

University of Chicago. *Women in the University of Chicago.* May, 1970. [ERIC ED 042537]

Indiana

AAUP (Bloomington). *Sex discrimination in Indiana colleges and universities: A survey.* November, 1972. [ERIC ED 074994]

Hardaway, C.W. *The status of women in the faculty of Indiana State University.* 1971. [ERIC ED 062958]

Indiana State University. *The status of faculty women at Indiana State University: A survey.* November, 1972. [ERIC ED 074994]

Indiana University (Bloomington). *Study of the status of women faculty at Indiana University, Bloomington Campus.* January, 1971. [ERIC ED 056632]

Kansas

AAUP (Emporia). *Report One of the Committee on the Status of Women.* 1970. [ERIC ED 043310]

University of Kansas, Lawrence. *Reports of Associated Women Students Commission on the Status of Women. 1969–1970.* 1970. [ERIC ED 043315]

Massachusetts

Boston State College Ad Hoc Committee on the Status of Women. *Report of the status of women faculty at Boston State College.* March 1972. [ERIC ED 074995]

Harvard University. *Preliminary report on the status of women at Harvard.* March, 1970. [ERIC ED 043299]

Harvard University. *Report of the Committee on the Status of Women in the Faculty of Arts and Sciences.* April, 1971. [ERIC ED 057714]

Maryland

Ingram, A. *Beliefs of women faculty about discrimination.* (University of Maryland) 1973. [ERIC ED 075005]

Sandler, B. *Sex discrimination at the University of Maryland.* 1969. [ERIC ED 041565]

Minnesota

Truax, A. and others. *Research on the status of faculty women, University of Minnesota.* May, 1970. [ERIC ED 041564]

University of Minnesota. *Report of the Subcommittee on Equal Opportunities for Faculty and Student Women.* April, 1971. [ERIC ED 056637]

Michigan

Michigan State University. *A compilation of data on faculty women and women enrolled at Michigan State University.* July, 1970. [ERIC ED 056630]

University of Michigan, Ann Arbor. *The higher the fewer. Report and recommendations: Committee to Study the Status of Women in Graduate Education and Later Careers.* Submitted to the Executive Board of the Graduate School, the University of Michigan, Ann Arbor, Michigan, March 1974. [ERIC ED 092024]

Wayne State University. *Today and tomorrow: Annual report of the Commission on the Status of Women.* August, 1972. [ERIC ED 073740]

New Jersey

National Organization for Women (Princeton Chapter). *A preliminary report on the status of women at Princeton University.* April, 1971. [ERIC ED 056634]

North Dakota

AAUP (Grand Forks). *The status of women at the University of North Dakota, 1971–1972.* May, 1972. [ERIC ED 078797]

Ohio

Bowling Green State University. *The status of women faculty at Bowling Green University.* May, 1972. [ERIC ED 066144]
Schoen, K.T. and others. *Report of the Ad Hoc Committee to Review the Status of women at Ohio State University, Phases I and II.* April, 1971. [ERIC ED 062959]
Van Fleet, D.D. *Salaries of males and females: A sample of conditions at the University of Akron.* December, 1970. [ERIC ED 056638]

Oregon

Acker, J. and others. *The status of women at the University of Oregon: Report of an ad hoc committee.* 1970. [ERIC ED 046335]

Pennsylvania

Carnegie-Mellon University. *Final report of the Commission on the Status and Needs of Women at Carnegie-Mellon University.* November, 1971. [ERIC ED 060799]
University of Pennsylvania. *Women faculty at the University of Pennsylvania.* March, 1971. [ERIC ED 056635]
University of Pittsburgh. *Advisory Council on Women's Opportunities. Progress report to the chancellor.* November, 1970. [ERIC ED 045054]
University of Pittsburgh. *Discrimination against women at the University of Pittsburgh.* November, 1970. [ERIC ED 049689]

Rhode Island

Lamphere, L. and others. *Report of the AAUP Committee on the Employment and Status of Women Faculty and Women Graduate Students at Brown.* October, 1970. [ERIC ED 045061]

Virginia

New University Conference, Hampton VA., Peninsula Chapter. *Women in Virginia Higher Education.* 1971. [ERIC ED 056639]

Washington

University of Washington. *Report on the status of women at the University of Washington: Part I: Faculty and staff.* October, 1970. [ERIC ED 045060]
Washington State University, Pullman, Commission on the Status of Women. *Report on the status of women.* February, 1972. [ERIC ED 078742]

Wisconsin

University of Wisconsin. *Final report on the status of academic women.* 1971. [ERIC ED 056633]
Van Dyk, J. & Freeman, B.C. *Preliminary report of the UW Faculty Women's Survey.* April, 1973. [ERIC ED 081356]

Index

AAUP (Bloomington), 105
AAUP (Denver), 104
AAUP (Emporia), 105
AAUP (Grand Forks), 106
Abramson, J., 75
Acker, J. *et al.*, 107
Acker, S., 57
Allen, I.L. & Wilkie, J.R., 75
Almquist, E.M., 21
Almquist, E.M. & Angrist, S., 21
Alper, T.G., 40
Alperson, E.D., 42
Andberg, W.L., 61
Angrist, S., 22
Arter, M.H., 68
Association of American Colleges, 42-43, 48
Astin, H., 58-59
Astin, H.S., 32, 85
Astin, H.S. & Bayer, A.E., 75
Astin, H.S. & Bisconti, A.S., 22
Astin, H.S. *et al.*, 12, 101
Athanassiades, J.C., 17
Attwood, C.L., 60

Babey-Brooke, M. & Amber, R.B., 105
Bailey, R.C. *et al.*, 40
Baird, L.L., 57
Barabas, J., 101
Baruch, G., 17
Bayer, A.E. & Astin, H.S., 75
Bell, J.B. & Bodden, B.F., 57
Bengelsdorf, W., 36
Benham, L., 51
Bergman, B.R. & Maxfield, M., Jr., 80
Berkowitz, T. *et al.*, 102
Bernard, J., 9
Bernstein, M.C. & Williams, L.G., 75

Bertelson, J., 28
Bisconti, A.S. & Astin, H.S., 49
Blackstone, T. & Fulton, O., 91
Blaska, B., 46
Blitz, R.C., 102
Boston State College Ad Hoc Committee on the Status of Women, 106
Boulding, E., 36
Bowling Green State University, 107
Brandenburg, J.B., 32
Bratfisch, V. *et al.*, 104
Bruce, J.D., 85
Brush, L.R., 29
Burstyn, J.N., 9
Business Week, 63

Carnegie Commission on Higher Education, 9, 103
Carnegie-Mellon University, 107
Cartter, A.M. & Ruhter, W.E., 59
Cartwright, L.K., 62
Centra, J.A., 59
Centra, J.A. & Kuykendall, N.M., 59
Chalmers, E.L., Jr., 12
Chemical and Engineering News, 90
Cherry, N., 22
Chmaj, B.E., 103
Chobot, D.S. *et al.*, 36
Chronicle of Higher Education, The, 61-62, 68
City University of New York, 105
City University of New York, Brooklyn College, 105
Clark, D.R., 80
Clifford, M.M. & Walster, E., 60
Coates, T. & Southern, M., 17
Coates, T.J. & Southern, M.J., 75

Connecticut Education
  Association, 104
Conway, J. & Jordan, P., 29
Conway, J.K., 9
Cope, R.G., 43
Counseling Psychologist, The, 52
Crawford, M.C. et al., 85
Cross, K.P., 33, 43-44
Curtis, R.C. et al., 17
Carnegie Commission on
  Higher Education, 9, 103
Carnegie-Mellon University, 107
Cartter, A.M. & Ruhter, W.E., 59
Cartwright, L.K., 62
Centra, J.A., 59
Centra, J.A. & Kuykendall, N.M., 59
Chalmers, E.L., Jr., 12
Chemical and Engineering News, 90
Cherry, N., 22
Chmaj, B.E., 103
Chobot, D.S. et al., 36
Chronicle of Higher Education, The, 61-62, 68
City University of New York, 105
City University of New York,
  Brooklyn College, 105
Clark, D.R., 80
Clifford, M.M. & Walster, E., 60
Coates, T. & Southern, M., 17
Coates, T.J. & Southern, M.J., 75
Connecticut Education
  Association, 104
Conway, J. & Jordan, P., 29
Conway, J.K., 9
Cope, R.G., 43
Counseling Psychologist, The, 52
Crawford, M.C. et al., 85
Cross, K.P., 33, 43-44
Curtis, R.C. et al., 17

Dahl, K.H., 105
Daniels, A.K., 57
Davis, S.O., 49

de Wolf, V. & Lunneborg, P.W., 33
Department of Labor Women's
  Bureau, 102
Deutrich, M.E., 85
Dickerson, K., 29
Divine, T.M., 81
Douvan, E., 17
Dube, W.F., 62
Durcholz, P. & O'Connor, J., 33

Eckert, R., 91
Edwards, J.N. & Klemmack, D.L., 22
Ekstrom, R.B., 36
Epstein, C.F., 12
Epstein, C.F. & Bronzaft, A.L., 23
Epstein, C.R., 68, 94
Epstein, G.F. & Bronzaft, A.L., 17
Etaugh, C. & Bowen, L., 29
Ewald, L.S., 37

Faia, M.A., 75
Farber, S., 75
Farley, J., 29
Farmer, H.S., 91
Farmer, H.S. & Bacher, T.E., 23
Faunce, P.S. & Loper, R.G., 44
Feldman, S.D., 57
Ferber, M. & Leob, J., 105
Ferber, M.A. & Huber, J.A., 75
Ferber, M.A. & Loeb, J.W., 91
Fields, C.M., 81
Fields, R., 86
Fisher, K.M., 104
Fitzpatrick, B., 37
Flanders, J., 76
Flora, C.B., 86
Francis, B., 105
Frankfort, R., 9
Freeman, B.F., 94
Freeman, J., 9, 12
Freivogel, E.F., 9

Friedman, B., 101
Frohreich, D.S., 49
Furniss, W.T. & Graham, P.A., 12

Gadzella, B.M. & Fournet, G.P., 40
Gardner, R.E., 49
Garman, L.G. & Plant, W.T., 57
Gearty, J.Z. & Milner, J.S., 44
Geisler, M.P. & Thrush, R.S., 33
Gillie, A., 30
Glass, K.D. & Schoch, E.W., 44
Goerss, K.v.W., 71
Goldman, R., 46
Goldstein, J.M., 76
Gordon, R.S. & Ball, P.G., 69
Graham, P.A., 9
Gray, M.W., 81
Green, A.A., 86
Greenfield, E., 81
Groszko, M. & Morgenstern, R., 37
Groth, N.J., 92
Gump, J.P., 18

Haines, J. & Penny, S., 69
Hall, D.T., 18
Hamovitch, W. & Morgenstern, R.D., 92
Hardaway, C.W., 105
Harlan, A. *et al.*, 92
Harmon, L., 23, 40, 101
Harris, A.S., 103
Hartnett, R.T., 71
Harvard University, 106
Hedges, L.V. & Majer, K., 50
Heilbrun, A.B., Jr., 40
Heins, M. *et al.*, 51
Helson, R., 10
Herman, M.H. & Sedlacek, W.E., 23
Hewitt, B.N. & Goldman, R.D., 41

Hochman, L.M. & Nietfeld, C.R., 60
Hoffer, S.N., 52
Hoffman, D. & Hoeflin, R., 24
Hollander, H.E. *et al.*, 94
Hollon, C.J. & Gemmill, G.R., 76
Holmstrom, E.I., 10
Holmstrom, E.I. & Holmstrom, R.W., 57
Horner, M., 41
Horner, M.S., 18, 68
Howard, S., 94
Howe, F., 13
Huber, J., 18
Hughes, H.M., 86
Hull, D., 33
Husbands, S., 30

Illinois State University (Normal), 105
Indiana State University, 105
Indiana University (Bloomington), 105
Ingram, A., 76, 106
Intellect, 62
Iowa Law Review, 49

Johnson, G.E. & Stafford, F.P., 76
Johnson, R.W., 24
Journal of the National Association for Women Deans, Administrators, and Counselors, The, 53

Karman, E.J., 24
Katz, J. *et al.*, 34
Kaufmann, S.G., 67
Kaye, B. & Scheele, A., 69
Keiffer, M.G. & Cullen, D.M., 77
Keller, B.B. & Chambers, J.L., 30
Kilson, M., 95

Kimmel, E.B., 82
Kjerulff, K.H. & Blood, M.R., 57
Knudsin, R.B., 92
Koch, J.V. & Chizmar, J.F., Jr., 77
Krenkel, N., 95

La Sorte, M.A., 86
Lamphere, L. *et al.*, 107
Lee, O.L. & Hall, J.E., 50
Lefevre, C., 58
Leland, C.A. & Lozoff, M.M., 30
Leslie, L.L., 37
Lester, D. & Lester, G., 30
Lester, R.A., 77
Lewin, A.Y. & Duchan, L., 87
Liebman, J.S., 87
Liss, L., 77
Littig, L.W., 42
Loeb, J. & Ferber, M., 77
Luchins, E.H., 87
Lundegren, H., 48
Luria, Z., 24
Lussier, V.L., 82

Mackay, M., 95, 104
Mackie, M., 78
Magarrel, J., 78
Magarrell, J., 38, 67
Marecek, J. & Frasch, C., 18
Masterman, M., 78
Mattfeld, J., 67
Maxwell, P. & Gonzalez, C., 19
Mayfield, B. & Nash, W.R., 78
McBee, M.L. & Suddick, D.E., 38
McCarthy, J.H. & Wolfe, D., 60
McCarty, P., 31
McEwen, M.K., 47
McGuigan, D.G., 10
McMillan, M.R., 25
McMillan, M.R. *et al.*, 24
Mednick, M.T.S. & Puryear, G.R., 19

Michigan State University, 106
Mickelson, S., 38
Mills, G.H., 101
Miner, J.B., 50
Minturn, L., 104
Mitchell, J.M. & Starr, R.R., 82
Montanelli, R.G., Jr. & Mamrak, S.A., 87
Moore, K.M., 31, 71
Moore, K.M. & Veres, H.C., 25
Moore, K.M. & Veres, H.C., 45
Moore, W.J. & Newman, R.J., 59
Mount Holyoke Alumnae Quarterly, 97
Muhich, D., 45
Mulligan, K.L., 34
Munley, P.H. *et al.*, 47
National Education Association, 67
National Educational Association, 96
National Organization for Women (Princeton Chapter), 106
New University Conference, 107
Newman, J.E., 58
Nichols, C.G., 34
Nies, J., 61
Notestine, E.B. & Kerlin, L., 25

O'Connell, A.N., 35
Occhionero, M.F., 39
Oliver, L.W., 19, 41, 47
Oltman, R.M., 13, 63, 95
Oster, R.G., 70
Ott, M.D., 50
Owens, N.J., 11

Parelius, A.P., 19
Parrish, J.B., 25, 63
Patterson, M., 31, 87
Patty, R.A., 19
Payton, L.C., 104
Peden, I.C. & Sloan, M.E., 82

112

Pennsylvania State Library, Harrisburg, 101
Perkins, J.A., 88
Peters, D.S., 78
Pfiffner, V.T., 72
Phelps, A.T. et al., 25
Pingree, S. & Butler-Paisley, M., 97
Pinson, C.B. & Caffrey, B., 92
Puryear, G.R. & Mednick, M.S., 42

Reagan, B.B., 88
Reagan, B.B. & Maynard. B.J., 82
Reeves, M.E., 67
Reid, E.A., 47
Rendel, M., 79
Reuben, E. & Hoffmann, L., 83
Rezler, A.G. & Buckley, J.M., 51
Rice, J.K. & Goering, M.C., 35
Richardson, M.S., 26
Richardson, M.S. et al., 26
Roberts, S., 79
Robinson, L.H., 13, 101
Roby, P., 11
Rogers, J.C., 20
Rose, H. & Elton, C., 26
Rosen, R.A.H., 63
Rossi, A.S., 88

Sandler, B., 11, 79, 83, 106
Sandmeyer, L. et al., 70
Schetlin, E.M., 67
Schmeller, K.R., 83
Schmidt, M.R., 31
Schoen, K.T. et al., 107
School Review, 54
Seater, B.B. & Ridgeway, C.L., 58
Sells, L.W., 61
Seltzer, M.M., 31
Sewell, W.H., 39
Sexton, P., 103
Shapiro, E. et al., 70

Shapley, D., 83
Sherman, R.G. & Jones, J.H., 27
Shoemaker, E.A. & McKeen, R.L., 79
Smith, D.E., 11
Smith, D.G., 41
Smith, G.M., 84
Solmon, L.C., 61
Sproule, B. & Mathis, H.F., 51
Standley, K. et al., 88
Stanford University School of Medicine, 104
Start, N. et al., 104
Stead, B.A., 88
Steele, C.M. & Green, S.G., 79
Steininger, M. & Eisenberg, E., 45
Steinmann, A., 20
Sternglanz, S.H. & Lyberger-Ficek, S., 31
Stiehm, J., 14
Streiker, A.B. & Johnson, J.E., 20
Strober, M.H., 63
Suter, B. & Domino, G., 45

Tangri, S.S., 27
Tanur, J.M. & Coser, R.L., 80
Ten Elshof, A. & Mehl, D., 41
Theodore, A., 84, 96
Thurston, A.J., 72
Tidball, M.E., 32, 93
Tidball, M.E. & Kistiakowsky, V., 84
Tittle, C.K. & Denker, E.R., 35
Touchter, J., & Shavlik, D., 70
Tournier, M., 11
Travis, C.B., 20
Travis, T.G., 84
Tresemer, D., 21
Trigg, L.J. & Perlman, D., 27
Truax, A. et al., 106
Turner, B.F. & McCaffrey, J.H., 27

United States Office of Education, 102
University of California, Berkeley, 48, 104
University of California, Santa Cruz, 104
University of Chicago, 105
University of Kansas, Lawrence, 105
University of Michigan Center for Continuing Education for Women, 14
University of Michigan, Ann Arbor, 106
University of Minnesota, 106
University of Pennsylvania, 107
University of Pittsburgh, 107
University of Washington, 107
University of Wisconsin, 108

Valentine, D. *et al.*, 27
Van Alstyne, C. *et al.*, 67
Van Dyk, J. & Freeman, B.C., 108
Van Fleet, D.D., 107
VanderWilt, R.B. & Klocke, R.A., 47
Veres, H.C., 28
Vetter, B.M., 89
Vetter, B.M. & Babco, E.L., 96
Voss, J.H. & Skinner, D.A., 21

Washington State University, 107
Wasserman, E. *et al.*, 85
Watkins, B., 89
Wayne State University, 106
Weissman, M.M. *et al.*, 97
Weitzman, L. *et al.*, 104
Wells, J.A., 35
Westervelt, E.M. & Fixter, D., 101
Weston, L.C. & Stein, S.L., 32
Weston, P.J. & Mednick, M.T., 43
White, B.E., 89

Wilcox, T., 89
Wild, C.L., 39
Williams, M. *et al.*, 71
Wilms, B., 35
Wilson, K.M., 46
Wolfe, J.C. *et al.*, 90
Wolfson, K.P., 28
Women's College Coalition, 95
Wood, M.A., 90
Woodhall, M., 52

Yale University, 104

Zelinsky, W., 90
Zell, L.C. & Weld, E.A., Jr., 39
Zuckerman, H. & Cole, J.R., 90